Addiction in Human Development
Developmental Perspectives on Addiction and Recovery

Jacqueline Wallen, PhD, MSW

The Haworth Press
New York • London • Norwood (Australia)

The Haworth Press, Inc., 10 Alice Street, Binghamton, NY 13904-1580

Library of Congress Cataloging-in-Publication Data

Wallen, Jacqueline.
    Addiction in human development : developmental perspectives on addiction and recovery / Jacqueline Wallen.
       p. cm.
    Includes bibliographical references and index.
    ISBN 1-56024-247-7 (alk. paper).
    1. Narcotic addicts – Psychology. 2. Alcoholics – Psychology. 3. Developmental psychology. I. Title.
RC564.W36 1992
616.86′001′9 – dc20

                                91-32981
                                  CIP

To Eric and Sara

ABOUT THE AUTHOR

Jacqueline Wallen, PhD, MSW, is Associate Professor in the Department of Family and Community Development of the University of Maryland at College Park. Previously, she was Assistant Chief of the Treatment Research Branch in the Division of Clinical and Prevention Research at the National Institute on Alcohol Abuse and Alcoholism. Dr. Wallen is a member of the National Association of Social Workers and the National Council on Family Relations.

CONTENTS

Preface

This is a book for substance abuse and mental health professionals who work with clients who have alcohol or drug problems. It
relates concepts from major theories of human development to the
problem of addiction and shows how a developmental perspective
can contribute to the understanding and treatment of alcoholism and
drug abuse. The approach taken in this book has evolved out of
courses in human development that I taught for the Washington
Area Council on Alcoholism and Drug Abuse (WACADA) for several years. A course in human development is required for certification as an addictions counselor in Washington, DC, as it is in many
states. This requirement reflects the growing recognition that alcoholism and drug addiction, and recovery from these problems, involve a number of developmental issues. First, an individual's development can be affected by the use of alcohol or drugs. Parental
abuse of alcohol or drugs may also affect an individual's development. It is important to be able to identify developmental deficits in
individuals with an individual or family history of alcohol or drug
abuse so that interventions for the substance abuse problem can also
address these deficits. Second, addictions have their own developmental course. Understanding how addictions develop gives the
mental health professional additional tools to interrupt addictive
patterns and prevent them from being passed from one generation to
the next. Third, recovery is itself a developmental process, with
identifiable stages. Professionals working with individuals in recovery can benefit from learning about these stages and assessing potential interventions to determine whether they are appropriate for
the individual's stage of recovery. Understanding the developmental issues that are of current importance to the client can also improve communication and rapport between helping professionals
and recovering individuals.

Though the students in the classes I taught were meeting requirements for certification as addictions counselors, most already worked in the area of substance abuse and quite a few had advanced degrees in psychology, social work, or other similar fields. They came from a wide variety of backgrounds, however. Some had stopped their formal education after high school. Others had earned equivalency degrees after dropping out of high school. A number were, themselves, recovering from alcohol or drug problems. They were all eager to apply theories of human development to their work and the questions that they asked reflected their desire for practical information. They wanted to know, for example, how individuals who had missed out on critical developmental milestones due to their dependence on alcohol and drugs could make up for lost time in recovery. They questioned the relevance of human development theories and research based on the experience of white, middle-class children in intact families and asked whether and how these principles could be applied to the experience of minorities and the poor or to the experience of children growing up in single parent families. Taking a course in human development also caused many students to become aware of developmental issues and traumas of their own. These realizations were often quite sudden and sometimes were accompanied by painful feelings of loss or anger that affected all of us. Sharing this process with students in the class increased my awareness of the strong connection between personal and professional growth.

Because students asked me to copy my notes for them, I began organizing and improving my notes so that I could distribute them. Each time I taught the class, I revised my notes and tried to make them more relevant to the questions and concerns that the students had raised in the previous class. After many repetitions of this process, the notes began to look more and more like a book. I presented parts of the book in workshops for private therapists and for mental health professionals working in agencies providing addiction and child protection services to assess its usefulness for these groups. These professionals also proved eager to review theories of human development and to learn about current research on human development and addiction treatment. They were particularly interested in the impact of childhood trauma on personality development and in the relationship between substance abuse problems and other mental health problems. They wanted to know whether the impact of childhood trauma on personality could be overcome and, in particular, how to help individuals who were recovering both from substance abuse and the delayed effects of childhood abuse. All seemed to feel that a developmental perspective applied as much to work with adults as it did to work with children.

Because I have presented parts of this book to classes and workshops as works-in-progress over the past several years, numerous people have helped to shape it. I would especially like to thank my students at WACADA's Center for Addictions Training and Education for providing a perfect mix of criticism, encouragement, and appreciation. I would also like to thank my friend, Nancy Doran, for her emotional support and for being very generous in sharing professional expertise and case material with me. Others who have shared case material and ideas include Kate Berman, Fulton Caldwell, Carol Hendler, and Bette Ann Weinstein. My editor at Haworth, Bruce Carruth, has a very light touch but gave me just the guidance I needed. My daughter, Sara, was a stellar copy machine operator. Writing this book has been an exciting experience for me and has made me feel grateful to the many teachers from whom I have had an opportunity to learn. Two in particular, Jerry Gerasimo and Fred Brewster, made a very big difference.

Eclectic) my Based on
view / Personal
Train to
date of
focus on
applied +
5, beh Δ

Introduction

WHAT IS A DEVELOPMENTAL PERSPECTIVE?

A developmental perspective focuses on how individuals change and grow throughout life and on the patterns and structures that shape their thoughts, feelings, and behaviors at any particular point in development. Human development as a discipline grew out of long-term studies of children's growth and behavior begun in the 1930s. As behavioral scientists increasingly recognized that human beings continue to develop and learn throughout life, the field of human development expanded beyond child development into the adult years and the process of aging. Even the process of death has been viewed as a developmental process (Kübler-Ross, 1969).

Most developmental theories stress the significance of earlier experiences in affecting later development, and assume that successful coping with any particular developmental event depends, at least in part, on the success with which an individual has resolved prior developmental issues. At the same time, most modern developmental theories are optimistic. They see growth and development as the natural tendency of the organism. Even when environmental circumstances are less than optimal, individuals do their best to learn and grow, often showing considerable resourcefulness. Often adult behaviors that seem "symptomatic" are in fact coping strategies that enabled the individual to survive hardships in childhood. This does not mean that optimal development is inevitable, but that individuals resolve each stage to the best of their abilities, given the resources they have available to them. Unresolved developmental issues may be carried along through life, however, and be an enduring weak point in character that detracts from the individual's ability to resolve subsequent challenges.

Some developmentalists use the concept of "developmental stage" to indicate that individuals at similar points in the life cycle

1

often have similar concerns, perceptions, feelings, and techniques for coping, even if their personalities are quite different from one another. At each stage, they face certain common developmental or "socio-emotional" tasks. These theories look for unifying patterns or organizing principles that influence behavior at various points in the life cycle and then use these concepts to define particular developmental stages. Though individuals do not all develop at the same rate, they do all pass through similar stages.

While there is great diversity among those who study human development, many, if not most, theorists embrace at least some of the following developmental concepts:

1. Individuals are motivated to learn and grow.
2. Development progresses through a fixed sequence of stages.
3. Rates of development vary among individuals.
4. Stages have specific socio-emotional tasks.
5. Each stage is a building block for later stages.
6. Unresolved tasks may become personality "themes."
7. The impact of life events is influenced by the developmental stage at which they occur.

A CASE ILLUSTRATION
OF DEVELOPMENTAL ISSUES IN RECOVERY

The following case illustrates a number of developmental issues in recovery.

Jim and Sandra Cutter are a married couple in their early 30s with two children, 11 and 9 years old. Jim is currently in his fifth week of a six-week inpatient alcoholism treatment program. Sandra is participating in a group for family members and patients. Jim, who has a college education, is a sergeant in the army and works as a recruiter, a position that requires him to be away from home most of the time, spending a total of perhaps 60 days at home in a year. He has just agreed, over Sandra's protests, to be reassigned to this position for another two years. Sandra dropped out of school at 17 and received a GED. She returned to school several years ago and recently completed a two-year business school program. She now works for a service that makes temporary secretarial placements.

Jim's decision to enter alcoholism treatment at this time was not really prompted by a concern about his drinking but rather by the fact that he had been using cocaine intravenously for the past year. He had become increasingly frightened by his heavy cocaine use and by the illicit activities (including selling drugs) that supported his cocaine habit. His constant travel away from home and his drug-dependent life style also involved him in numerous extramarital encounters and affairs. In the past year he had contracted several serious venereal diseases.

Sandra also has experienced problems related to her drinking. She states that once she starts drinking, she never knows what is going to happen. Sometimes she is able to drink moderately, other times she drinks until she passes out. She has experienced blackouts and has vomited in her sleep after passing out. She has abstained from alcohol since Jim entered alcoholism treatment and acknowledges that she has a drinking problem, but says that she does not want to label herself as an alcoholic and feels that she can take care of her drinking problem on her own.

Sandra is an attractive woman with brown eyes and shoulder-length brown hair. She is intelligent and articulate, but seems somewhat shy. Though she shows little emotion, even when discussing painful events in her life, she has several distinctive mannerisms that appear when she talks about topics that distress her. She twists her fingers together and a muscle in her neck twitches visibly, pulling down the corner of her mouth for a moment. Jim is tall and slender and wears wire-rimmed glasses that give him a rather intellectual appearance. His left ear has been pierced three times but he no longer wears earrings in it. Jim, like Sandra, is intelligent and well-spoken, but he has a slightly arrogant manner and tends to disparage Sandra when she shows enthusiasm or when she looks to him for affirmation. For example, Sandra told the family group proudly that when Jim visited home for the weekend she had made a huge pitcher of fresh lemonade so that there would be an appetizing non-alcoholic drink in the refrigerator. Jim seemed at first not to remember the lemonade. When Sandra continued to insist that he must remember, he finally said, "Oh, yeah. I didn't drink that. I prefer iced tea.'' Sandra responds to such remarks by lowering her eyes and becoming silent.

Jim's father died several months ago. Both Jim and Sandra are uncharacteristically emotional when Jim's father is discussed, crying at the mention of his name. They say that Jim's father is the only relative on either side of the family that they felt close to. He was also the only person to accept and support their marriage. Other family members disapproved because Jim is black and Sandra is white. Jim and Sandra refer to Jim's father as Jim's "enabler," however, meaning that he facilitated Jim's alcohol and drug use by intervening and protecting him whenever Jim had problems because of them. He also encouraged Jim to drink with him from an early age.

Sandra describes herself as a "loner" since childhood and has few social contacts and no close friends. This year she has begun to form some tentative relationships outside the home. Her son takes karate classes and participates in competitions. Her daughter studies jazz dance and also performs competitively. Sandra enjoys attending their classes and events, using these as opportunities to socialize with the other parents. She is even beginning to think about taking some dance classes herself.

This is Jim's first and Sandra's second marriage. Sandra became pregnant for the first time when she was 15, and, although she did not want to, her mother convinced her to marry the father of the baby. The marriage lasted for a year and a half before Sandra moved back home with her mother and stepfather, bringing the baby with her. About a year later, Sandra married Jim, leaving her daughter in North Carolina with her mother. Her daughter, who still lives with Sandra's mother and stepfather, is now 17 and has dropped out of school. Sandra believes her daughter has a drinking problem and attributes her daughter's problems to Sandra's mother's failure to discipline her.

Sandra's father, who is actively alcoholic and has a history of compulsive gambling, was divorced from Sandra's mother when Sandra was seven. Sandra's mother remarried soon after, to a man who had four children of his own. Sandra's stepfather worked for an oil company, and they moved often throughout the rest of her childhood. About two years ago, Sandra, who had not seen her biological father since the divorce, decided to find her father and establish contact with him. She says that she was motivated primarily by a feeling that she had no real relationship with her mother and by a fantasy that the father she found would be the idealized father she remembered from early childhood. In fact, her father was destitute and practically homeless, living in a motel. When Sandra located him, she impulsively invited him to come and stay with them until he could find a job. He moved in almost immediately and has made no effort to find a job or to become independent of Jim and Sandra. He does not really function as a family member, but instead isolates himself in his room, which he has stripped bare of furniture except for a mattress and some milk crates. He keeps a six pack of beer on his windowsill and uses the empty cans for ashtrays. Sandra is angry at her father for taking advantage of them and would like him to leave but cannot bring herself to tell him so. In the meantime, she and the children interact with him as little as possible. When they do interact with him, it is with a degree of contempt. This concerns Sandra because she feels it communicates negative values to her children about relationships.

Sandra says that her mother spent very little time with her when she was a child and that there was almost nothing about her that her mother approved of. She recalls her mother calling her "stupid," "fat," and "clumsy." She says her mother wanted her to be a socialite and a Southern belle, while she preferred reading and being alone. Sandra has not seen her mother since she was married, although she does speak to her on the phone. Sandra feels that she cannot visit her mother because her mother disapproves of her marriage to Jim. Sandra's mother has pictures of Sandra's sister and her husband and two children on a wall of her home. Alongside these pictures, she also has pictures of her four stepchildren and their families. She has no pictures of Sandra, Jim, or their children and has told Sandra that she does not want people to see that her daughter is married to a black man. Sandra also has a very distant relationship with her sister. All the other family members, including the stepchildren, are very close to one another and see each other often.

Jim is the youngest of eight children. He had an especially close relationship with his father, while his next oldest brother, Jeff, has always been his mother's favorite. Jim is resentful of Jeff because he feels his mother treats Jeff with the nurturance due a youngest child while this position really belongs to Jim. He also holds Jeff responsible for their father's death. He says Jeff made no attempt to revive their father after the heart attack that resulted in his death and that Jeff did not call the rescue service as quickly as he should have. Jeff and several other brothers of Jim's have drug problems. One died of an overdose this past year. Another "found Christ," according to Jim, and stopped using drugs. Jeff still does use drugs.

A number of developmental issues stand out in the Cutter family's story. The Cutters can be described as being in a particular developmental stage, both as individuals and as a family. Also, they are in particular stages of recovery, again, both individually and as a family. In addition, they approach treatment with a number of unresolved developmental tasks.

Stage of Recovery

At the present time, Sandra and Jim have only partially accepted their respective alcohol and drug problems. Jim is quite clear about his desire to stop using drugs, but although he denies it, he gives the definite impression that he feels he can probably continue to use alcohol as long as he does not use drugs. Sandra acknowledges that she has been drinking too much, but still feels that she can control her drinking. Neither Jim nor Sandra have fully acknowledged the extent of their substance abuse problems. In Chapter 2, recovery as a developmental process is discussed in greater detail.

Developmental Stage

The Cutters, as individuals, are in the developmental stage that Erik Erikson has called "Generativity vs. Self-Absorption" (Erikson, 1963). In this stage, a married couple must establish and maintain a pattern of divided labor and shared living that enables them to maintain their family unit and nurture and guide their children, if they have children. Sandra has been able to make the developmental transition to parenthood, but the Cutters have been unable, as a couple, to resolve their life cycle task of maintaining a home and parenting their latency-aged children together. Jim's alcohol and drug problems, along with his absence from the home, have been significant factors standing in the way of their resolving this important task. Sandra says that she and Jim were very close and harmonious before the children were born. Their time was spent drinking and partying together. After the children were born, Sandra focused on the home while Jim continued in their previous life style, becoming more and more peripheral to the family. Also standing in the way are earlier developmental tasks that remain unresolved for both Jim and Sandra. For example, Jim and Sandra's intimacy early in the relationship depended very heavily on drinking and partying together rather than on getting to know and accept one another as individuals. As such, it was a kind of "pseudo-intimacy." Their marriage has never been accepted by Sandra's family and achieved only limited acceptance from Jim's family. They have never really cemented their existence as a couple. Chapter 4 further discusses the issue of family life cycle stages.

Unresolved Developmental Tasks

The Cutters' failure to bond as a couple reflects a failure to complete fully the developmental tasks of late adolescence, which include developing a positive identity for oneself without either completely rejecting or remaining enmeshed in one's family of origin. Both Jim and Sandra are still struggling with powerful needs for recognition and affirmation from their own parents. They have not differentiated themselves sufficiently from their families of origin. The next chapter presents a conceptual framework for understanding uncompleted or unresolved developmental tasks.

REFERENCES

Erikson, E. H. (1963) *Childhood and Society*. NY: W. W. Norton.
Kübler-Ross, E. (1969) *On Death and Dying*. NY: Macmillan.

Chapter 1

Developmental Issues in Recovery

A colleague of mine recently told me a story that illustrates how important a sensitivity to developmental issues can be when working with individuals who have alcohol or drug problems:

> Irma had been referred for an assessment to determine whether she should continue receiving disability payments. A victim of severe childhood physical and sexual abuse, she was receiving disability payments because of an anxiety disorder which prevented her from working. She had been placed on an anti-anxiety medication by her physician.
>
> Irma was a few months away from her sixtieth birthday, but she looked at least ten years older. The information she gave in response to questions about her drinking indicated that she also suffered from longstanding alcoholism. My colleague, reluctant to "enable" Irma's alcoholism by signing the disability form without addressing her drinking problem, suggested that she continue in therapy to resolve some of the issues underlying her anxiety problems and that she attend an open Alcoholics Anonymous meeting to explore the possibility of working on her drinking problem. While Irma indicated that she was willing to continue in therapy for her anxiety disorder, she made it clear that she would terminate therapy if she were pressed further on the issue of her drinking. The therapist agreed to continue to see Irma for therapy but, after several more weeks, did press Irma further on the question of attending an AA meeting, at which point Irma terminated therapy.

Shortly after Irma terminated therapy, my colleague received a pamphlet from the Johnson Institute in the mail. The Johnson Institute is known for its pioneering work in developing techniques for intervention and confrontation with alcoholics. An intervention is a technique for persuading an alcoholic to accept treatment. In an intervention, individuals who play an important role in the alcoholic's life (family members, employers, friends), after much planning and with the guidance of a trained professional, confront the alcoholic with their perceptions of her behavior and insist that she seek treatment. The pamphlet stressed that interventions with older individuals must proceed differently from interventions with younger people. In particular, they must be conducted much more slowly. This therapist said that if she had been aware of the special needs of older alcoholics, she would not have expected to address her client's alcohol problem so quickly.

An individual's current developmental stage affects how she experiences interventions for her alcoholism or drug abuse. Problems in recovery are also influenced by developmental stage. For this reason, it is necessary to be aware of the developmental issues that are currently most salient for the individual being treated for substance abuse. Because unresolved developmental issues from the past also affect recovery, it is also important to assess the extent to which conflicts or deficits originating in earlier development stages are still active in influencing feelings and behavior.

Psychodynamic approaches, including psychoanalytic theory, and neo-Freudian perspectives such as the object-relations school, ego psychology, and self theory, provide a comprehensive framework for understanding developmental stages.

PSYCHODYNAMIC VIEWS OF DEVELOPMENT

Psychodynamic theories focus not just on behavior, but also on the emotional processes underlying behavior, especially motives for behavior. Many of these underlying processes are unconscious. They originate in the interaction between developmental and environmental influences.

While there are a number of different psychodynamic approaches to development, most have been influenced in some way by the psychoanalytic approach originating in the work of Sigmund Freud. Freud based his theory on the existence of inborn drives that underlie human behavior. These drives can be seen as a kind of energy in the sense that when they are unsatisfied, they build up and lead to a kind of tension, or uncomfortable excitation in the organism. Because humans, like all other organisms, are motivated to maximize pleasure and to minimize pain, we respond to this tension with activities aimed at reducing it. The most straightforward way to reduce tension is simply to meet the need. For example, a hungry infant can reduce tension resulting from her hunger by nursing. Whatever we focus on as having the potential to meet the drive we are currently experiencing is, in Freudian terms, the object of that drive. For the very young infant, the object of her hunger is the bottle or the breast, whichever is the usual vehicle for her nourishment. Freud actually pictured the drive, or energy, attaching itself to the object, or "cathecting" the object. He believed there were two basic drives: Eros (sexual or erotic energy, or libido) and Thanatos (aggressive or destructive energy), but his developmental theory focuses more on libido than on aggression.

While individuals are motivated to gratify their inborn drives, society is based on the individual's ability to control them. In this sense, human nature and civilization are at odds. Social organization would be destroyed if individuals indulged all of their sexual and aggressive urges. Because human beings require the care and protection that societies offer in order to survive, we must learn to reconcile our instinctual drives with the limitations society places on meeting them. Individuals with alcohol and drug problems, in many ways, dramatize this conflict. They have become accustomed to gratifying needs in a way that often puts them at odds with society.

The internalized representation of the inevitable conflict between the individual and society has been described by Freud in terms of a three-part model of the psyche. The id, for Freud, consists of the instinctual drives, mostly unconscious, that motivate human behavior. The superego is made up of the restrictions placed by society, particularly through parental influence, on gratifying these unconscious drives. These restrictions are internalized by the individual **and produce an uncomfortable or perhaps painful feeling of guilt** when the individual violates them or even thinks about violating them. The ego is the part of personality that enables the individual to meet instinctual needs within the constraints imposed by the superego and by the external environment. The ego, for example, may postpone gratifying a physical desire until an appropriate time, may substitute a socially acceptable pleasure for an unacceptable one, or may repress an unacceptable urge. These are all called ego defenses because they are mechanisms employed by the ego to defend the individual against pain while still meeting instinctual needs. While the ego has a defensive function, it also has a survival function. It is responsible for coping with reality – both inner and outer. The more primitive the ego defense used by the ego (that is, the earlier in development it originates), the more it obscures reality and interferes with coping. A strong, healthy ego is one that can accommodate to reality. In Freud's terms, it functions according to the "reality principle." Individuals with alcohol and drug problems often have problems in this area. Ego strength is achieved through coping with the challenges that life inevitably presents. To the extent that an individual has turned to alcohol or drugs to allay painful feelings instead of learning to cope with stressful experiences, that individual has been deprived of opportunities to build ego strength. In addition, by relying on alcohol, they have avoided the need to develop more differentiated, sophisticated ego defenses.

Most defenses are based, at least to some extent, on the mechanism of repression, which involves keeping forbidden urges unconscious. Repression facilitates a number of different kinds of defenses. Different psychodynamic theorists tend to stress different defenses, but all agree that defenses that dominate early in development are more primitive (more global and undifferentiated) than those developing later on. This has to do primarily with cognitive factors. The infant cannot perform complex mental operations. As a result, the psychological defenses employed by an infant must be very simple and rudimentary. The most primitive defense discussed by Freud is one he terms denial. Denial involves denying an unpleasant fact or aspect of external reality that interferes with instinctual gratification through fantasy or in behavior. One way that an infant can deny reality is to go to sleep. Harry Stack Sullivan calls this "somnolent detachment" (1953).

Another way that the infant can deny reality, according to Freud, is to engage in "primary process" thinking. In primary process thinking, the infant gratifies a need in fantasy that it cannot gratify in reality. The existence of primary process thinking has never actually been proven to exist in infants, but the concept remains a useful metaphor for thought processes that clearly occur in adults. Many drug-induced states, for example, reflect primary process thinking rather than an attempt to cope with reality.

While defenses based on denial can relieve tension, denial, by definition, involves ignoring reality. Reliance on denial, therefore, can interfere with ego development because it deprives the ego of information that would enable it to accommodate to and cope with inner and outer reality. As a rule, the more developmentally primitive the defense, the more it is based on repressing or denying reality. Projection, in which an individual attributes a forbidden wish or impulse of her own to someone else, is another defense that develops relatively early in development. In projection, reality is not completely denied. The drive and the obstacles to its fulfillment are acknowledged, but the locus of the drive is misperceived.

Defenses that evolve later in development are more sophisticated and differentiated. These defenses allow more aspects of reality to be taken into account. In contrast to denial and projection, sublimation is a highly sophisticated defense mechanism. It involves substituting a similar, but socially acceptable, activity for a forbidden one. The impulse is acknowledged and transformed into a socially useful or culturally valued behavior. The more developmentally advanced the defense, the more likely it is to produce socially valued, or "civilized" behavior in the individual. For example, an individual might sublimate aggression by participating in a competitive sport. Or he might sublimate sexual urges by creating sculptures of the human body. In sublimating their sexual and aggressive urges, humans have produced great art, literature, and music, and have created highly evolved civilizations.

Rationalization is another fairly sophisticated defense that the individual does not become capable of until fairly late in development. Rationalization consists of providing a reasonable intellectual justification for an unacceptable urge or behavior. It is advanced because it is reality-based and because it uses thought and reasoning. It is more primitive than sublimation, however, because the individual still acts on the forbidden impulse rather than transforming it into a more acceptable behavior.

Two defenses that develop in early childhood, but after infancy, are identification and reaction-formation. They are more advanced than such infantile defenses as denial and projection because they involve accommodation to reality. They also may produce socially valued behaviors, although this is not always the case. Identification involves gratifying a need symbolically or vicariously by identifying with another whom one considers successful in this regard. Reaction-formation occurs when one overemphasizes a feeling opposite to the forbidden one. Both defenses provide an impetus to growth and development when they motivate an individual to adopt prosocial, rather than antisocial, attitudes and behaviors.

Freud argued that the primacy of the genital zone in sexuality was only a relatively late feature in human development. He introduced the notion of infantile sexuality, calling the infant "polymorphously perverse." By this he meant that the infant can derive libidinal satisfaction from many different kinds of stimulation. In fact, the story of human development is the story of the sequential emergence of a series of erogenous zones, each posing a developmental conflict that the individual must resolve. Freud believed that mental disorders arise in the course of the development of an individual's sexual instincts and reflect fixation, or developmental arrest, at certain stages in development during which the individual could not fully resolve the developmental tasks posed. Under stress, an individual predisposed to mental disorder may regress to that point in development where fixation occurred, manifesting behavior that bears the hallmark of that period.

While Freud's theory focused rather narrowly on this aspect of the infant's experience, many modern psychodynamic theorists have broadened the classical perspective on infancy to include a wide range of experiences. Comparing traditional Freudian theory to neo-Freudian ego psychology, Stephen Johnson discusses the distinction between "conflict models" and "deficit models" of ego development or developmental arrest (1987). Freud's is a conflict model. It holds that development is shaped by how an individual resolves conflicting impulses, drives, or feelings at each stage of life. Developmental arrest occurs at points in development where these conflicts cannot be resolved and can be remediated only through uncovering and resolving these conflicts. A deficit model, more characteristic of ego psychology, or self theory, emphasizes developmental deficits rather than conflicts. In this view, developmental problems may often be resolved by strengthening the ego functions that were not initially adequate.

In working with individuals recovering from alcohol or drug problems, it is important to be able to apply both models. Virtually all individuals who have used alcohol or drugs to such an extent that one or both have become a problem in their lives have some developmental deficits. These deficits may be contributing factors in their continuing reliance on alcohol or drugs, a result of this dependence, or, more likely, both. Many of these deficits can be remedied through providing information or opportunities to learn new skills. Individuals who have never learned to deal with anxiety without alcohol or drugs, for example, can benefit from learning techniques for relaxation and stress reduction. Individuals who learned to "stuff" their anger by getting drunk instead of trying to change problem situations may profit from assertiveness training. Other areas in which recovering individuals may need information or skills include parenting, financial management, social relationships, communication, and sexuality.

Sometimes what has been missed is experiential and cannot be taught in this manner: the experience of cooperating in a group, for example; the experience of trusting another with one's feelings; or the experience of coping successfully with a set of structured requirements. Some opportunities for overcoming these experiential deficits can be provided in substance abuse treatment, some in therapy, and others in Alcoholics Anonymous or other self-help groups.

When neither education nor experiential opportunities seem to help remedy a deficit, then the existence of an underlying conflict can be suspected. In these cases, psychotherapeutic techniques for dealing with unconscious conflict are appropriate.

Types of Developmental Issues in Recovery

1. Issues Connected to Current Life Stage
2. Deficits or Vulnerabilities that Originate in Earlier Life Stages

- Information or skills deficits
- Experiential deficits
- Unconscious conflicts/fixation

ERIKSON'S STAGES OF DEVELOPMENT

Erik Erikson, an ego psychologist, focuses on ego strengths and deficits in development. He also emphasizes the importance of the child's social environment in shaping development. Like Freud, he identifies stages in development, but for Erikson, developmental themes are primarily "psychosocial," rather than "psychosexual," meaning that social rather than sexual issues are of key importance in shaping personality. Erikson characterizes each developmental stage in terms of the primary task or psychosocial issue that must be resolved in that stage. He also draws on the work of object-relations theorists who emphasize the critical importance of the child's relationship to the parenting figure in the first few years of life. His eight stages of development are helpful tools for the clinician. They are easy to remember and describe the key issues of each developmental stage.

Erikson's Developmental Stages

Trust vs. Mistrust
Autonomy vs. Shame and Doubt
Initiative vs. Guilt
Industry vs. Inferiority
Identity vs. Role Diffusion
Intimacy vs. Isolation
Generativity vs. Self-Absorption
Integrity vs. Despair

Trust vs. Mistrust

Freud called this period the "oral stage" because he considered the oral region (involving sucking and biting) to be a focal point for libidinal energy in the infant. This stage is characterized by Erikson in terms of what he considers to be the basic task of this period: the development of "basic trust." The alternative is a failure of trust, or "basic mistrust."

According to object-relations theorists, the ability to sustain intimate relationships — ones in which the other is loved for himself or herself rather than being seen simply as an object one uses to meet one's own needs — depends on a series of developments that begin in infancy. This process begins with the infant becoming attached to the parenting figure because the parent represents a source of need gratification. This relationship is initially completely narcissistic, or self-centered. Narcissistic attachment, or bonding, to a nurturing parent figure is a hallmark of normal development in infancy. Infants who are unable to develop such an attachment may manifest other developmental problems such as "failure to thrive." If the mother (or primary parenting figure) is "good enough" (Winnicott, 1965), however, the infant is able to form an attachment or bond and the bond gradually generalizes out to the point where the infant bonds with others as well.

Through the experience of being successfully parented, the infant learns to trust that its needs will be met and feels secure. Later it will be able to acknowledge that others have a separate existence and needs of their own. This forms the basis for true intimacy, or give and take, between the individual and others.

Melanie Klein is an object-relations theorist who strongly emphasizes the importance of the first year of the infant's life. She talks about some of the stresses that are involved for the infant, even when it receives "good enough" mothering (Klein, 1984). Even the best of mothers is not always instantly available. Sometimes the bottle is too hot or the nipple is plugged up and the infant must wait. To an infant this is extremely upsetting, perhaps even terrifying. Infants do not have the same kind of defenses that we do or the same kind of time perspective. They have no sense of object permanence. A delay may feel like total abandonment. The infant may experience overwhelming anxiety. Denial has already been discussed as a defense mechanism available to the infant. Another defense, described in detail by Klein, has been called "splitting." The infant may experience the gratifying mother and the ungratifying mother as two different mothers: the good mother and the bad mother. If the infant frequently experiences frustration or abandonment, these two figures may remain split in his or her experience. This is a very primitive kind of defense that may cause the infant to have severe problems later on. It is, in Erikson's terms, a failure to complete the task of developing "basic trust." Basic trust involves knowing that even though frustrations occur, and parents are not always perfect, they are basically reliable and consistent and can be counted on. Continuity in parenting also helps the infant develop a trust in the continuity of self.

Reliable parenting, combined with the development of a rudimentary concept of object permanence at around eight months, permits the infant to begin to develop ways of behaving that enhance the likelihood of receiving gratification from the parent. According to Bowlby and others who emphasize the importance of infancy in development, these models, or attachment behaviors can become characteristic patterns of relating to others, and the attitudes developed in early relationships often become enduring expectations.

If there are problems in the parent-child bond, then children may also be deprived of a number of mechanisms typically learned in infancy through receiving "good enough" mothering that could later help them deal with stress and other unpleasant feelings. One such mechanism has been termed "self-soothing." Children who are adequately comforted by a parent when upset eventually learn to comfort or soothe themselves when they feel frustrated or afraid. This ability is part of what Erikson means by basic trust. Paul Horton, a psychiatrist, has related adequate comforting in childhood to the ability to be receptive to spiritual solace as an adult (1981). Other signs of ego strength, such as the ability to defer gratification or to tolerate anxiety or frustration, also may originate in the sense of trust that results from the experience of receiving "good enough" parenting in infancy.

Recovering individuals with developmental deficits originating in infancy may face issues of concern in recovery that are analogous to those of the period of "trust vs. mistrust." These include intense fears of abandonment, the inability to tolerate anxiety or to engage in "self-soothing" behaviors, and difficulties with intimate relationships. Alcohol or drugs may have been used to cope with these inadequacies.

Whether a recovering individual's difficulties reflect deep-seated personality traits or simply deficits in information or coping techniques, there are a number of tools with which they can be provided. Stress-reduction and relaxation techniques, meditation, and guided imagery are all useful in reducing anxiety. Guided imagery can also be used to remedy some experiential deficits. For example, imagery in which the client encounters and comforts his or her own inner "wounded child" can help the client learn to "self-soothe" or "self-parent." Other experiences that can be both self-nurturing and anxiety-reducing include massage and other kinds of body work (such as acupuncture) and meditative exercise techniques such as tai chi or yoga. The structure and emotional support provided by AA meetings and by AA-related reading materials can also be extremely helpful.

One client was able to understand and counteract his pattern of recurrent relapse by becoming aware of his inability to comfort and nurture himself and by learning ways to meet these needs without alcohol:

> A 45-year-old computer programmer, Steven had been hospitalized for alcoholism treatment three times in the past six years. Each time, he left treatment committed to maintaining his sobriety and immersed himself in a demanding regimen of 60-hour work weeks and daily AA meetings. On Sundays he attended three AA meetings. While participating in a Relapse Prevention group during yet another hospitalization, Steven realized that his relapses had always followed a predictable pattern. Though his demanding program of work and AA left Steven little time to think about drinking when he first left treatment, he would eventually become weary of the unrelieved monotony of his daily grind. He would begin to wonder what the point was in staying sober if this was all there was to life. Eventually he would decide to cut down on his work hours and to reduce his attendance at AA meetings, but, because he had no idea of how to amuse or enjoy himself except by drinking, he would eventually begin filling his free time by dropping into bars. After this, it was only a matter of time before he lost his job or was arrested for driving while intoxicated and landed back in treatment.

Steven needed to learn how to structure his time to include both work and leisure and how to relax and enjoy himself without drinking. He learned to use audio tapes for relaxation and also renewed his interest in building model ships. Rather than force himself into a frenetic round of AA meetings, he picked several meetings to attend regularly and concentrated on developing friendships within these meetings. For the first time, he got a sponsor. From his sponsor, he learned how to use the AA "HALT-Stress" technique, remembering to ask himself, whenever he was out-of-sorts, "Am I *H*ungry, *A*ngry, *L*onely, or *T*ired?" and then taking appropriate action by eating, talking about his anger to his sponsor, seeking companionship from a friend, or going to bed. Previously, the only way he knew to take care of himself had been to take a drink.

As the infant begins to crawl and walk, she ventures farther from the parent, trusting the parent to be there. Some parents have difficulty validating their child as a separate person.

Alice Miller, a psychoanalyst, describes adult patients of hers who, on the surface, seem to have had safe, protected, perhaps even idyllic childhoods, yet suffer from depression and are unable to achieve intimacy with others (1981). Miller feels that these are individuals who, although they had all of their physical needs met, were "narcissistically deprived" in childhood, in that they did not receive unconditional love and respect for themselves. Drawing on object-relations theory and self theory, Miller argues that the child has "a primary need to be regarded and respected as the person he really is at any given time, and as the center — the central actor — in his own activity." This includes all of the infant's emotions, sensations, and behaviors. Consistent with these theories, Miller believes that if the child is loved and validated for himself, he will be secure enough in his feelings about himself and his relationship to his mother to gradually move away from her and establish his own separate identity.

When the child's narcissistic needs are not met, the result is what has been called a "narcissistic disturbance." The child has been deprived of respect, echoing, understanding, sympathy, and mirroring, even though its basic needs may have been met. This has consequences for adulthood. Miller has observed that her patients, as adults, still have difficulty experiencing the kinds of feelings that would, in childhood, have threatened the parent. The individual may still be very vulnerable to feelings of abandonment and may feel that he has to present an "as-if" personality, or "false self" (Winnicott, 1965). The individual cannot develop and differentiate a true self because he is unable to express those feelings or behaviors that he feels are unacceptable. In a sense, the individual remains psychologically tied to parents or to other "significant others" because he cannot rely on his own emotions. He has not learned about them through the trial and error of acting on them and observing the consequences, and has no sense of his own real needs. He is alienated from himself and, because he cannot separate from his parents, he remains as an adult dependent upon affirmation from others: his partner, the groups to which he belongs, and his own children (Miller, 1981).

Autonomy vs. Shame and Doubt

In the anal stage, for Freud, the anal region becomes an important site for sexual tensions and gratifications. Toilet training is an issue that results in the attribution of a great deal of importance to the child's feces. Defecating is a pleasurable experience, but withholding feces may also be pleasurable. Where, when, and how the child will defecate becomes an important control issue between parents and children. It is during this stage that parents begin to have definite expectations concerning the child's behavior and the child begins to internalize parental attitudes about good and bad, right and wrong, clean and dirty, etc. Reaction-formation may be an important defense in the anal period.

Erikson calls this period the stage of autonomy vs. shame and doubt. Consistent with his psychosocial emphasis, Erikson places less stress on toilet training itself during this stage, and more stress on the question of autonomy and control. The two-year-old child is far more mobile and adventurous than the infant. Also, we expect more of a toddler than we do of a baby. "No" may be the word this child hears most frequently during the day as she explores, experiments, and challenges the limits and boundaries placed on her. The child who has an adequate sense of basic trust will be able to venture out somewhat independently of the parents, knowing the parents will be available when needed. If the limits placed on the child at this stage are too severe or harsh, however, she may lose confidence in her ability to cope with the world around her. If she is made to feel ashamed of her failures (for example, toilet training accidents), she may develop a sense of shame about herself—a sense that there is something wrong with her as a person. A child who does not come to this period with a sense of basic trust may have problems developing a sense of autonomy. Without the faith that she has someone to fall back on, she may not trust herself to venture out into the wider environment.

Issues in recovery that are analogous to those of this period include problems with self-identity, self-esteem, and self-worth as well as the problem of shame.

> Donna entered recovery with shame directly related to the issue of toilet training. When she was three, her mother had punished her for wetting her pants by making her sit on the front porch all afternoon with her plastic potty hanging from her neck on a string. Throughout her childhood, long after her last toilet training accident, her mother put plastic sheets on her bed "because Donna wets her bed."

> Randy was a 30-year-old biologist who had been forbidden by his mother to play with the boys in his neighborhood after he knocked out a tooth rough-housing with a friend when he was four years old. His mother decided at that time that the boys in the neighborhood were too wild and, from then on, only allowed him to play with the girls. He remembered, with great shame and embarrassment, playing with the girls on the front lawn of the house next door while the boys rattled down the sidewalk on their noisy "Big Wheel" tricycles. As an adult, Randy attributed his feelings of inadequacy and self-hate to his destructive alcoholic binges. In recovery, however, he felt overwhelmed by diffuse and painful feelings of shame that he could no longer contain by blaming them on his drinking.

Even in families where child-rearing is more benign, shame can be an issue. Fossum and Mason, in their book *Facing Shame: Families in Recovery* (1986) point out that shame is an inevitable component of family systems organized around addiction. For the child of the addicted parent, as well as the addicted individual, the addiction is accompanied by secretiveness and shame, as well as denial and attempts to relieve shame by projecting blame onto others. Alcohol or drugs may be the cause of the shame, but also the means for containing and relieving it. When recovering individuals become abstinent, they may suffer from the loss of a focus for their self-blame and may be flooded with feelings of self-hate and shame for which there is no apparent present cause. Twelve-step programs such as Alcoholics Anonymous and Alanon provide a setting in which individuals can share experiences and feelings that have produced shame in the past and gain acceptance from other group members who have had similar problems. The group context is a particularly useful setting for overcoming shame.

Initiative vs. Guilt

For Freud, the phallic stage is the stage during which limits imposed by others truly begin to be internalized by the child to form a conscience, or superego. In the child between the ages of approximately four and six, sexual energy becomes concentrated in genitals. The crisis that shapes the superego involves a cluster of events and feelings that Freud called the Oedipal complex after Oedipus, the Greek tragic hero who murdered his father and married his mother. Freud believed that as the phallic area becomes an erogenous zone for the boy, he begins to fantasize about eliminating his father and marrying his mother. Fearing that his father knows about these feelings, the boy also fears that his father will castrate him in retribution. To defend himself, the boy identifies with his father. (Freud has called this phenomenon "identification with the aggressor.") This serves the dual purpose of satisfying the father (who is pleased with the boy's imitative behavior) and giving the boy the opportunity to symbolically or vicariously possess the mother through his identification with the father. In internalizing the father, the boy is internalizing his father's authority, thus creating a superego. Freud felt that the strength of the superego reflected, at least in part, the degree of fear the boy felt toward his father.

In the girl, the process is slightly different, according to Freud. Although the girl also fantasizes about having an exclusive relationship with her father, she does not need to be as afraid of her mother as a boy might be of his father. First of all, the mother is probably less powerful than the father. Also, the girl does not have the "castration anxiety" that a boy experiences because she does not have a penis. Her problem is "penis envy" and the fact that she must reconcile herself to the fact that she feels less valuable because she does not have a penis. When she "identifies with the aggressor" (e.g., her mother) to possess her father symbolically, she is identifying with someone whom she also sees as less valuable because her mother also lacks a penis. Because he saw fear as a less important factor in the formation of girls' superegos, Freud felt that girls did not ever develop quite as strong a conscience as boys did.

Needless to say, Freud's perspective has numerous detractors. One of the critics of the masculine bias so apparent in Freud's description of the Oedipal crisis, Carol Gilligan, has pointed out that while the developmental differences described by Freud no doubt do result in distinctive male and female superego characteristics, there is no justification for assuming that men, therefore, have superior superegos (1982). The fact that separation from the mother is critical to male development but not so important for girls means that girls shape their superego in the context of their relationship to their mother, imitating her attitudes of caring and responsibility. Boys shape their superegos through separating from their mother and identifying with a powerful person whom they also fear. This may explain why, where moral judgments are concerned, males tend to be more concerned with rules and rights, while females are more concerned with situational contexts and responsibilities. Neither one style nor the other is necessarily better, however. In fact, Gilligan argues that the highest form of morality would combine both.

When Erikson describes the Oedipal period, he refers to the task of initiative vs. guilt, and again he highlights more general psychosocial issues than Freud. In this case he points to the active imagination and energy that characterize four- and five-year-old children. This is the age, especially in boys, of preoccupation with super-heroes and other symbols of power and mastery. Girls, too, may identify with such figures or they may identify with traditional symbols of female power and may "mother" their dolls, play house, or dress up. Boys at this age also like toys that remind them of their father's power in the family — toy lawnmowers or power tools, etc. This is not to say that male and female children always identify with parents in such traditional and sex-stereotyped ways, though Erikson, like Freud, presents a relatively sex-stereotyped picture of development. While gender identity does affect development, a girl may imitate the father and aspire to the kind of power he has in the family. The boy may also imitate the mother. Furthermore, families differ from one another in how they organize family responsibilities. In one family the father may do most of the cooking and the mother may be responsible for repairs or both parents may share a range of responsibilities. In many families the mother raises her children alone and must model adult behavior for both male and female children. The most important factor may be which parental behaviors are most observable to the child. Children identify readily with the concrete behaviors they observe daily. Their identification with parental behaviors they hear about but do not observe, such as parents' work, may be weaker and more abstract.

In any event, it is important that the child at this stage identify with the significant adults in the family and be supported in the fantasy of someday achieving adult privileges. At the same time, limits must be set, but not in such a way that they cause the child to feel excessively guilty about his fantasies and ambitions. When this stage is successfully negotiated, the child will identify with the parents, particularly the same sex parent, and will be optimistic about the future, accepting the necessary limitations of the present. If limits are too severe, or if limits are not imposed at all, the child may feel guilty or hopeless.

Issues reminiscent of this period that surface in recovery may have much of the flavor of the original Oedipal crisis and may include issues of sexuality and sexual identity, especially if parental sexual boundaries were unclear. Sexual abuse experienced during

this period may be remembered or become especially salient in recovery (see Chapter 3).

> Martin was the 36-year-old son of two alcoholic parents.
> During his childhood, Martin's parents' marriage was charac-
> terized by frequent and violent fighting provoked by Martin's
> father's extramarital affairs. During these fights, Martin's
> mother would often threaten to leave Martin's father and in
> many cases would go so far as to ask Martin which parent he
> wanted to stay with when she and Martin's father divorced.
> Martin was flattered by his mother's attempts to win him over
> but was afraid of losing his father. He would plead with his
> parents to stay together and assumed, throughout his child-
> hood, that it was his efforts at mediation that held the marriage
> together. When he was 20, Martin married a woman ten years
> his senior. Very shortly after their marriage, she insisted that
> he enter treatment for his alcohol and drug problems. He com-
> plied, and was able to remain abstinent for the next five years,
> at which time she left him because of his compulsive extra-
> marital affairs. At this time, on the advice of his therapist,
> Martin became involved in a 12-Step program that focused on
> compulsive sexuality.

As a child, Martin was repeatedly torn between the fantasy of having his mother all to himself and the fantasy that he could reunite his
parents. In his marriage, he acted out this conflict with affairs that
antagonized his wife, whom he convinced each time not to leave
him. Martin was eventually able to remain faithful in a relationship
while also remaining alcohol and drug free. Another client, Wendy,
was unable to maintain relationships with men without using alcohol and drugs.

> Wendy and her father had been especially close throughout
> her childhood, though Wendy's father often teased her about
> her weight, telling her that if she didn't lose weight, no man
> would ever want to marry her. At the same time, he disap-
> proved of the men she dated. In his eyes, none of them were
> good enough for her. At 29, Wendy, who was also a heavy
> drinker, smoked marijuana throughout the day, beginning in
> the morning before she went to work. She was an extremely

successful sales manager for a computer company, and felt that her marijuana smoking enhanced her work performance rather than impairing it, but she periodically stopped drinking and using marijuana for months at a time in order to control her weight. She felt that she ate more when she was smoking marijuana than when she abstained. Drinking also caused her to gain weight. When she did abstain from alcohol and drugs, she lost weight, but found herself so anxious in relation to men that she would eventually begin to drink and use drugs again in order to relax on dates. Within a short period of time she would again be drinking heavily and smoking marijuana before going to work in the morning.

Wendy had internalized her father's implied message that she should avoid other men and used alcohol and drugs, along with overeating, to protect herself from relationships.

Industry vs. Inferiority

The next period in development, for Freud, is latency, which lasts from about six years old until puberty. During this period the child represses many sexual urges, often using the defense of sublimation. Instinctual drives are channelled into such socially acceptable activities as school work, sports, and play.

Erikson describes this as the period of industry vs. inferiority. Having accepted the fact that he must defer some of his dreams and fantasies until adulthood, the school-aged child ideally turns to the tasks of childhood — school and play — and is able to achieve some degree of success within this framework. To the extent that the child's efforts to succeed are rewarded, he will be reinforced in his sense of himself as a valuable and competent person. If the child is unable to achieve success, either because of his own limitations or because of characteristics of his environment, he may come to think of himself as less worthwhile or less able. This is the period in childhood when larger systems beyond the family have an increased impact on the child. Even the child who has developed a strong sense of self-worth and competence in the family may have difficulty if his school experience or peer relationships do not provide the opportunity for accomplishments that strengthen his sense of self. Social injustices such as racism, sexism, or economic inequalities may affect a child's ability to succeed in the school or the neighborhood during these years, in spite of the child's best efforts. As a result, he may find himself discouraged and lose confidence in his ability to succeed.

Children participate in organized activities with their peers during this period, and the games they play prepare them to cooperate and follow rules. They develop their ability to empathize and share (see Appendix C for a more detailed discussion of this process).

Issues related to this stage include the ability to sublimate, to function in groups, and to cope with competition. Achievement, motivation, and learning problems that have their origins in this period may again become significant in recovery.

When Brian decided to enter inpatient treatment for his cocaine addiction, he called a treatment center to find out how much the treatment program would cost and then went out and sold enough cocaine to pay for it. A 32-year-old black man from an established upper-middle class family, Brian had an Ivy-league college education and spoke a number of languages, some of them acquired through a stint with the Peace Corps in the Middle East. A nice, likeable, easy-going, accommodating person, Brian was characterized by his counselor as "chameleon-like." His counselors and other members of his group suspected that though he was cooperative, he was just going through the motions and was not really revealing himself. Though they confronted him on this, his presentation of self was seamless, and they were unable to penetrate it until it was Brian's turn to read his autobiography.

Listening to Brian's autobiography, which was a fairly straightforward account of the life of an upper-middle class youth and young man, his counselor was struck by how innocuous Brian's story was and how singularly lacking in anger of any kind. Being a black man himself, the counselor felt something was missing. How can a black man, even a relatively advantaged one, grow up in a racist society and tell such a bland story of his coming of age?

Part way through Brian's reading, the counselor interrupted him and asked him how he felt about being black. Brian responded that, to him, it was no big deal. He felt it really had not had a big effect on his life. Still troubled, the counselor interrupted him again a few minutes later and asked the same question. Again, Brian responded that, for him, it had not been an issue of any particular importance. After still more reading, the counselor asked again how he felt about being black. Brian exploded with anger. Jumping to his feet, Brian exploded, saying, "Goddamn mad about it, that's how I feel." He followed this with an outpouring of anger and pain, describing how belittled and blocked he had felt growing into manhood in a society that places less value on black men than on white men. With what his counselor described as a primal scream of pure rage, he picked up the heavy chair in which he had been sitting and threw it the length of the long room. His counselor had someone retrieve the chair, sat Brian down in it, and held Brian while he sobbed. After this experience, Brian's treatment turned around. Now, eight years later, he is still drug and alcohol free. Though he is no longer "Mr. Nice Guy," he is well-liked and professionally successful. Brian's dependence on drugs had enabled him to sidestep some of the painful developmental issues involved in developing a sense of self-worth in relationships with peers as a young black male in our society.

A number of individuals who become attracted to drugs and alcohol during the junior high or high school years have learning disabilities that make school achievement difficult and unrewarding. They learn to rely on alcohol and drugs or substance-abusing peers for their sense of well-being and fail to develop motivation and work patterns that support success in an educational or work setting. Recovering individuals with such a background are handicapped and can benefit from a specialized assessment of their learning style and possible learning disabilities. Some may require long-term vocational rehabilitation. Without a reasonable chance of vocational success, these individuals may have little motivation to remain free of drugs and alcohol.

Identity vs. Role Diffusion

Freud saw adulthood primarily in terms of the maturation of genital sexuality. In puberty, provoked by sexual maturation, many of the issues of the phallic, or Oedipal, period seem to return. These issues are not only sexual, acording to Erikson. The adolescent experiences a strong desire to possess all of the options and resources that the parents appear to have and may have intense clashes with parents, especially the same-sex parent. The individual at this age is beginning to think about the role she will have as an adult and seeks to define her identity through experimenting with a number of identities, attitudes, and roles. This experimentation may cause conflict with the parents, especially when the adolescent allies herself with friends, groups, or values that the parents consider dangerous or that they disapprove of. The adolescent's struggle for a meaningful identity also involves developing a sense of her place in the social order and requires a faith that the conventional order can provide meaningful rewards. In this sense it is somewhat of a replay of the "trust vs. mistrust" conflict but this time the adolescent is considering the issue of trusting herself and the wider society rather than simply trusting herself and a parent. The individual who is able to resolve the demands of this period will have a sense of who she is and of which adult roles might be meaningful and gratifying for her. If the demands cannot be resolved, the individual will remain confused about who she is and what she wants out of life.

The fact that the individual typically becomes capable of abstract logical reasoning during this period combines with the individual's struggle for individuation, or differentiation, to produce much of the turmoil of adolescence. Erikson points out that adolescents, with their ability to think critically, are often highly judgmental and sensitive to the hypocrisy that underlies much conventional social behavior. A risk of this period is that the adolescent will organize an identity around antisocial, rather than prosocial, behavior. Peer influence is of great importance at this stage.

Peer group participation and influence, educational and vocational goals, internalized standards for behavior, sexuality and sexual identity are all issues reminiscent of this period that may emerge in recovery.

Carl, an attractive 26-year-old who looked considerably younger, was in an inpatient alcoholism treatment program. Clearly above average in intelligence, he had attended part of one year of college after he left high school but had failed all of his first-semester courses and had never tried to return to school. He attributed his failure to his drinking. He said that he had associated with a heavy-drinking crowd during his last years of high school, but by the time he was in college, he drank so heavily that even his friends could not keep up with him and he spent much of his time in his room, drinking alone. Since his attempt at college, he had drifted from one temporary job to another, mostly gravitating toward jobs that permitted him to bring several six-packs of beer to work. At the time he entered treatment, he was working as a carpet-layer. Carl's father, an advertising executive who had retired and gone into business for himself, had died suddenly of a heart attack during Carl's senior year of high school. Carl was present when his father had the heart attack and had attempted to administer cardiopulmonary resuscitation but was unsuccessful in reviving his father. Carl's relationship with his father had been filled with conflict during the two years preceding the heart attack. Carl's father disapproved of his life style and friends, while Carl ignored his father and refused to accept his authority. At the time, Carl, whose father's business had not been very successful, considered his father to be a failure. In treatment, Carl spoke of his father and expressed guilt about his treatment of his father. He also mentioned that he felt he had never really permitted himself the opportunity to grieve his father's death. Because he was the only child still living at home when his father died, he had taken responsibility for managing the funeral and other matters. Soon after that, he had gone away to college and begun his heavy drinking.

Carl was encouraged to allow himself to experience some of the feelings that he had avoided when his father died and was asked to write a letter to his father, telling him how he felt about him. Carl took the assignment seriously and spent several weeks writing the letter, which he read aloud, crying in a few places. In the letter, he told his father that he loved him and asked for his forgiveness. He also told his father that he had quit drinking and that he planned to register in the local junior college when he completed treatment. When he was asked to imagine his father responding to the letter, Carl imagined his father telling him that it was all right and that he understood and was proud of him. This exercise relieved Carl of much of his guilt toward his father and allowed him to experience previously repressed feelings of grief about his father's death.

Intimacy vs. Isolation

In the next stage, which Erikson labelled intimacy vs. isolation, individuals are still struggling with the problem of differentiating themselves from their parents and establishing an independent identity for themselves. The intense friendships and attractions of adolescence pave the way for intimate love relationships in this period. Erikson felt that an intimate relationship with a partner depends on the resolution of the task of the previous stage — identity. Without a firm sense of who one is and what one's boundaries are, one cannot risk the blurring of boundaries that comes with intimacy. Furthermore, intimate relationships will call up many of the feelings an individual has about his parents. To the extent that the individual was not able to establish an identity of his own with regard to his parents, he will find himself reliving many of the same conflicts with his partner that he had with his parents.

Issues from this period that come up in treatment include intimate relationships, differentiation from parents, and sexual dysfunction.

Joan was a 40-year-old married women with a 16-year-old daughter who sought counselling for depression and marital problems through the employee assistance program at her place of work. Questions by her counselor revealed that she had a number of physical ailments for which she took an assortment of prescription painkillers and muscle relaxants and that she drank heavily each evening. She had seen various therapists in the past, but had never brought up her dependence on prescription drugs and alcohol because she feared that if she stopped using them, she would no longer be able to tolerate her marriage.

With her counselor's encouragement, she began attending

AA meetings and was able to discontinue both her alcohol use and her use of prescription drugs. As she had feared, however, she became more discontented with her marriage, even though her husband was supportive of her and stopped drinking in the evenings himself. Though she did not feel she could express this to her husband, she felt her marriage lacked the intimacy and excitement she longed for and was dissatisfied with her house, which she felt was too small and shabby, and with her husband's lack of financial success. She was still quite emotionally dependent on her parents and resented the fact that the couple frequently had to turn to them for financial assistance. Her counselor recommended a marriage counselor with experience in substance abuse treatment. With the assistance of the marriage counselor, Joan was forced to think through the demands she was making on her husband, and to voice some of her expectations. In doing this, she was able to recognize how romantic and unrealistic some of her expectations had been. She was able to negotiate with her husband to get other demands met. While this was occurring, she began taking more responsibility in other areas as well. She entered a training program to help her advance in her career and she and her husband went to credit counselors to learn how to manage the money they did have more effectively. As their financial situation improved, they were able to become financially independent of Joan's parents and to improve their house so that it met Joan's standards. Joan accepted the fact that her marriage would rarely be as exciting as the relationships she read about in romance novels, but was able to make some realistic demands on her husband that increased her satisfaction with the marriage.

Generativity vs. Self-Absorption

Freud did not perceive adult development as continuing past the point where genital maturity was achieved. Erikson distinguished several further stages of adult development, however. The first he called generativity vs. self-absorption. A developmental task encountered by most, though not all, adults is parenthood. Parenthood requires that the individual be able to put aside her own needs sufficiently to nurture and care for a child. The way in which an individual was nurtured by her own parents may affect her ability to nurture her own child. Parenting provides the individual with an opportunity to care for and create something outside herself, to make a contribution to the world that will still be there even after she is gone. The alternative is a narcissistic focus on self, which Erikson conceives of as a kind of stagnation. It is not necessary for a person to have a child in order to resolve the developmental issues of this period. Any kind of altruistic or socially useful commitment can serve the same purpose in that it enables the individual to go beyond the self to make a larger contribution. Devotion to a career, for example, can allow for generativity, as can dedication to some hobby or philanthropic goal. Being a therapist or a substance abuse counselor or helping fellow alcoholics through Alcoholics Anonymous all can involve generativity.

Alcohol can impair an individual's ability to parent or to be "generative" in Erikson's sense of the word.

> Marla was a 26-year-old woman whose six-year-old daughter, Lisa, had been placed in foster care by protective services because she had been sexually abused by one of Marla's boyfriends. Marla's relationship to her daughter was that of a peer, rather than a mother. Her daughter was her best friend and confidante. Marla, who was a heavy user of both alcohol and cocaine, was required by the court to submit weekly urine samples to establish that she was not using drugs. She complied with this requirement by submitting samples of her daughter's urine rather than her own. She was allowed to visit her daughter only under supervision by a social worker and was unable to understand why the social worker would not permit her to spend these visits in a bar. Marla's daughter was eventually placed with an adoptive family.

Some recovering chemically dependent parents are prepared to commit themselves to nurturing their children but lack parenting skills because they themselves were not adequately parented. Such parents can benefit from parent education classes and from opportunities to interact with and observe other parents. Those who experienced severe neglect or abuse in childhood may need to learn to care for and nurture themselves first, in order to parent their children appropriately. Other recovering parents seem unable to even make the commitment to care for their children. For Jim Cutter, described in the previous chapter, his abandonment of his parental role was tied to his inability to surrender his playboy bachelor life style. When asked in the family group how he though his drinking and drug use had affected his children, Jim nodded at his wife, Sandra, and said, "Oh, she takes care of that."

Chapter 5 presents greater detail on parenting problems in recovering substance abusers.

Integrity vs. Despair

In this final developmental stage, the earlier issue of trust vs. mistrust re-emerges at a much broader level. The question the individual must resolve is whether she trusts the whole process of life and death, and whether she sees the universe itself as safe and trustworthy. This may entail a life review in which she reviews her life and becomes reconciled to whatever path it has taken. She may need or want to tell the story of her life – in writing or to another person. An individual who has successfully completed the tasks of this stage is able to remain hopeful in the face of aging and the prospect of death and to perceive life as worth living. An individual who cannot resolve the issues of this stage may suffer from depression, bitterness about the past, or anxiety about the future.

Some special recovery-related considerations for older individuals were discussed earlier in this chapter as they related to the case of Irma. Older individuals typically approach recovery at a much slower pace than younger individuals. This is partly because they move through life more slowly, generally, than the young, but it also reflects the fact that they have had many more years to strengthen their defenses. It also may be more difficult for them to acknowledge their substance abuse problem, particularly if they are long-time abusers. So much of their life has been premised on the cognitive structure that maintained their denial that to abandon it at this point may threaten to make their life appear meaningless, just at a time when it is so important for them to attribute some value and coherence to the life they have lived.

Change, in general, can be difficult for the elderly. It is important to remember, as well, that the present generation of elderly may have quite different values and conceptions of what is appropriate than the post-World War II cohort. Today's elderly population did not grow up with the "let it all hang out" mentality that has characterized the past several decades. Topics that are now openly discussed on television were taboo when those who are now elderly were coming of age. They may not be comfortable with either the language or the content of AA meetings and may be repelled by group sessions in which participants are expected to share their personal problems. Social isolation is a major contributing factor to alcohol problems among the elderly, particularly when the alcoholism is of relatively late onset (perhaps after the death of a spouse or companion), and groups may be of great value to the elderly in recovery. These groups are often more successful, however, if they are recreational or social groups, or groups that focus on a particular interest (such as history, writing, or crafts) rather than therapy or AA groups.

SPIRITUAL DEVELOPMENT AND "DETACHMENT"

Erikson did not discuss death and dying in great detail, but Elisabeth Kübler-Ross has shown that there are developmental stages even within the process of dying. Kübler-Ross began her work on death and dying at the University of Chicago, where she developed a seminar for medical students, theological students, and other health care workers. Based on interviews with individuals who had terminal illnesses, she defined five stages in coping with death. They are denial, anger, bargaining, depression, and acceptance.

Kübler-Ross's stages have also been used to characterize the adjustment or grieving process that occurs whenever an individual experiences the loss of something of value. This may include not just the death of oneself or another, but the loss of a period of one's life, the loss of an aspect of one's self-image, or the loss of a substance to which one was addicted, for example, alcohol or drugs.

Judith Viorst, in a book heavily influenced by psychoanalytic theory entitled *Necessary Losses*, has put forth the view that all development implies loss. Among these losses she includes everything we have to let go of to change and grow: attachments, illusions, expectations, and aspects of ourselves that are no longer appropriate or that stand in the way of new ways of thinking or behaving. These are the "necessary losses" referred to in the title of her book.

Rather than seeing detachment as a reaction to loss, Carl Jung saw it as an important stage in development. Jung disagreed with Freud regarding the role of instinctual drives in shaping development and argued that individuals also have spiritual needs, and that these needs are as much a part of human motivation as are physiological needs. While Freud believed that psychological problems, or neuroses, stemmed from the conflict between instinctual drives and cultural restraints on their satisfaction, Jung believed that mental suffering could also be seen as resulting from a failure to meet spiritual needs. Freud helped his patients to analyze their dreams to reveal unconscious desires. Jung helped his patients to understand the spiritual concepts contained in their dreams and in other symbols they produced. Jung also placed far more emphasis than Freud on development in the second half of life, stressing what he called the process of "individuation." Individuation is the process by which the individual becomes uniquely himself or herself. Maslow referred to it as "self-actualization."

Abraham Maslow introduced the notion of a "hierarchy of needs" in the 1960s. He distinguished between two kinds of needs. The first kind he called "deficiency needs" and the second "being needs" or "growth needs."

Deficiency needs are "essentially deficits in the organism, empty holes, so to speak, which must be filled up for health's sake and furthermore must be filled from without by human beings other than the subject" (Maslow, 1968).

Psychologists had traditionally seen these needs as motivating behavior. They consist of: physiological needs (hunger, thirst), safety needs, and needs for belongingness and self-esteem. These needs operate hierarchically in that, when lower level needs are satisfied, they cease to motivate behavior and higher level needs become more important. Still higher in the hierarchy are growth needs, or "being" needs. These needs involve a drive toward self-actualization. They do not strive for homeostasis or tension-reduction, as lower level needs do. Instead, they may cause the individual to seek tension or disequilibrium.

Maslow studied "self-actualizers," or individuals who had achieved a level of achievement and success in the world that went well beyond the satisfaction of basic physiological or emotional needs. For example, he studied nationally recognized scientists. He found that self-actualizers were motivated far more by "being needs" than "deficiency needs." He also found that self-actualizers frequently reported the occurrence of what he called "peak experiences." A peak experience is a mystical or transcendent experience in which the individual feels herself to be valuable, good, and worthwhile. Such an experience may involve feelings of wonder and awe and a sense of the unity of the universe. In a peak experience, the individual's sense of ego or self may disappear but, paradoxically, Maslow has found that it is individuals with the strongest egos who are most likely to have a peak experience in which the ego is transcended.

In later writings (1970), Maslow also introduced the notion of a "plateau-experience." A plateau experience is a more low-key, less intense, more enduring sense of sacredness and unity or of the specialness of existence. Such an emotional or cognitive state is more contemplative and less dramatic than a peak experience. It might also be called "serenity." While peak experiences seem to appear serendipitously, plateau experiences can be earned through work, discipline, study, and commitment to a spiritual practice.

Maslow's conception of a "third psychology" or "third force" in psychology that studied "self-actualization" as well as pathology, provided the framework for a psychological perspective that came to be called "humanistic psychology." Humanistic psychology has been concerned with including "being" needs in theories of human behavior and has now been recognized by the American Psychological Association as a legitimate branch of psychology.

"Transpersonal psychology" represents a further outgrowth of the "third force" in psychology, which explicitly focuses on spiritual development. It is interdisciplinary and integrates traditional spiritual teachings with modern psychology. In contrast to humanistic psychology, this perspective has not yet received official ac-knowledgement from the American Psychological Association. Transpersonal psychology is an approach to mental health that goes beyond what is commonly accepted as normal to stress the value of transcending the ego to develop higher levels of consciousness (such as "peak" or "plateau" experiences). In a sense, this can be seen as transcending the "social self," shaped through our social experiences, to experience reality as it really is, without imposing our own needs and cognitive categories on it. Some transpersonal psychologists refer to a "Higher Self," or an inner spiritual core, that can be tapped once the "social self" is transcended. The field of transpersonal psychology has special relevance to the field of substance abuse treatment because substance abuse treatment has traditionally stressed participation in Alcoholics Anonymous or Narcotics Anonymous, programs that emphasize spirituality as an important element in the process of recovery from dependence on alcohol or drugs.

Howard Clinebell has developed a list of spiritual needs that may be considered a part of human nature:

1. The need for regular renewal of "basic trust," the awareness that life is trustworthy in some fundamental sense in spite of its tragedy and loss.
2. The need for sound values to undergird responsible relation-ships and a workable philosophy of life which gives purpose to living.
3. The need for a relationship with and commitment to an inte-grating object of devotion.
4. The need for regular energizing experiences of transcendence in which we can know and celebrate the essential goodness of life.
5. The need to move regularly from the alienation of guilt to reconciliation and forgiveness.
6. The need for the regular renewal of self-acceptance and self-esteem.
7. The need for the renewal of realistic hope and a sense of the possibilities of the future.

8. The need to discover and develop one's higher self as the integrating center of one's life.
9. The need to maintain nurturing interaction with nature and with humankind.
10. The need for a caring community committed to spiritual values.

Clinebell believes that a recognition of the individual's spiritual needs is especially important in addictions treatment. Research suggests that, at least as far as alcoholics' self-reports are concerned, recovering alcoholics, whether or not they have received formal substance abuse treatment, often mention religious or spiritual experiences in conjunction with their recovery. In one study of recovering alcoholics, Magruder-Habib et al. (1989) found that approximately 20 percent of the subjects mentioned religion as an important factor in maintaining their sobriety. Approximately the same proportion (21 percent) reported that they were ethically or religiously better off since they had quit drinking. Bill Wilson, the founder of Alcoholics Anonymous (AA), credited Carl Jung with the notion that a spiritual or religious experience could bring about recovery in alcoholism and felt that this principle was the foundation for the program he was instrumental in establishing (Kurtz, 1979). Wilson was also influenced by the psychologist and philosopher William James, who attributed the appeal of alcohol to its power to stimulate a mystical consciousness or sense of oneness with the universe. In *The Varieties of Religious Experience* (1967), James observed that:

> Sobriety diminishes, discriminates, and says no; drunkenness expands, unites, and says yes. It is in fact the great exciter of the *Yes* function in man. It brings its votary from the chill periphery of things to the radiant core. It makes him for the moment one with the truth. (pp. 304-305)

The notion of a spiritual awakening to the existence of a "higher power" is central to the Twelve Steps that form the core of AA. While the definition "higher power" is left up to the individual, Bill Wilson was insistent in his belief that a spiritual experience, whether sudden or gradual, was a major part of the experience of recovery in AA. The original handbook of AA, *Alcoholics Anonymous* (1976), states that:

> With few exceptions, our members find that they have tapped an unsuspected inner resource which they presently identify with their own conception of a Power greater than themselves. Most of us think that this awareness of a Power greater than ourselves is the essence of a spiritual experience.

The Twelve Steps of Alcoholics Anonymous are as follows:

1. We admitted we were powerless over alcohol — that our lives had become unmanageable.
2. Came to believe that a Power greater than ourselves could restore us to sanity.
3. Made a decision to turn our will and our lives over to the care of God as we understood Him.
4. Made a searching and fearless moral inventory of ourselves.
5. Admitted to God, to ourselves, and to another human being the exact nature of our wrongs.
6. Were entirely ready to have God remove all these defects of character.
7. Humbly asked Him to remove our shortcomings.
8. Made a list of all persons we had harmed, and became willing to make amends to them.
9. Made direct amends to such people wherever possible, except when to do so would injure them or others.
10. Continued to take personal inventory and when we were wrong promptly admitted it.
11. Sought through prayer and meditation to improve our conscious contact with God, as we understood Him, praying only for knowledge of His will for us and the power to carry that out.
12. Having had a spiritual awakening as the result of these steps, we tried to carry this message to alcoholics, and to practice these principles in all our affairs.

John had been raised as a Mormon but was excommunicated because of his alcoholism and his irresponsible life style, at which time his wife, who was also a Mormon, divorced him. Chastened, John sought treatment for his alcoholism and, after several years of sobriety, remarried his wife. At this time his wife, his wife's family, and his parents all put a great deal of pressure on John to return to the church. While John did eventually return to the Mormon church, it was only after several more years of exploring his religious identity, something he had never done when he originally belonged to the Mormon church. During these years of exploration and through participating in AA, John felt that he developed an inner spirituality that he had never experienced in his early years as a Mormon.

Recovering individuals who have connected to the spiritual aspects of recovery may find themselves troubled by experiences that they would have at one time perceived as morally neutral.

Rhonda was a young woman who had worked as a prostitute for four years to support herself and her cocaine addiction. During this time she was physically abused by her lovers and had numerous abortions. In recovery, Rhonda was able to give up prostitution, as well as alcohol and drugs, and became involved in a stable relationship with a man who cared for her and for whom she could also feel love. When she became pregnant, she had no reservations about having an abortion. She had never had any feelings or regrets at all about the abortions she had had in the past. This time however, she was devastated by the experience and suffered a brief relapse. In looking back on the experience she realized that she had come to have a much different view of life. This time, the abortion represented a loss that she had strong feelings about. It was no longer a casual act.

While spiritual growth can be an unexpected benefit of a program of recovery, as well as a bonus for professionals working in the field of addictions, it is by no means a universally shared experience for recovering individuals, nor is it necessary to recovery for all individuals. Even when recovering individuals relate strongly to the concept of a "Higher Power," they may define that higher power in terms of concepts that have little or nothing to do with conventional religious points of view.

REFERENCES

Alcoholics Anonymous (1976) NY: Alcoholics Anonymous World Services, Inc.

Clinebell, H. (1981) "The Role of Religion in the Prevention and Treatment of Addictions – The Growth Counselling Perspective," in *Man, Drugs, and Society – Current Perspectives: Proceedings of the First Pan-Pacific Conference on Drugs and Alcohol*, 206-213. Canberra: The Australian Foundation on Alcoholism and Drug Dependence.

Erikson, E.H. (1963) *Childhood and Society*. NY: W.W. Norton.

Fossum, M. and Mason, M. (1986) *Facing Shame: Families in Recovery*. NY: W.W. Norton.

Gilligan, C. (1982) *In Another Voice*. Cambridge, MA: Harvard University Press.

Horton, P.C. (1981) *Solace*. Chicago: University of Chicago Press.

James, W. (1967) *The Varieties of Religious Experience*. NY: Collier Books.

Johnson, S. (1987) *Humanizing the Narcissistic Style*. NY: W.W. Norton.

Jung, C.C. (1971) *The Portable Jung*. Joseph Campbell, ed. NY: The Viking Press.

Klein, M. (1984) *Contributions to Psychoanalysis, 1921-1945*. London: Hogarth Press.

Kübler-Ross, E. (1969) *On Death and Dying*. NY: Macmillan.

Kurtz, E. (1979) *Not-God. A History of Alcoholics Anonymous*. Center City, MN: Hazelden.

Magruder-Habib, K., Stevens, H.A., Saunders, W.B., Alling, W.C., and Willson, D.C. (1989) "Spontaneous Remission from Alcoholism," Paper presented at the Natural Course of Drinking: Implications for Public Health, Program on Alcohol Issues, University of California, San Diego.

Maslow, A.H. (1968) *Toward a Psychology of Being*. Second Edition. Princeton, NJ: Van Nostrand.

Maslow, A.H. (1970) *Religions, Values, and Peak-Experiences*. NY: Penguin Books.

Miller, A. (1981) *The Drama of the Gifted Child*. NY: Basic Books.

Sullivan, H.S. (1953) *The Interpersonal Theory of Psychiatry*. NY: W.W. Norton.

Viorst, J. (1987) *Necessary Losses*. NY: Ballantine Books.

Winnicott, D.W. (1965) *Maturational Processes and the Facilitating Environment*. NY: International Universities Press.

Chapter 2

Recovery As a Developmental Process

Brother Paul was a member of a religious order and had, for many years, been the director of campus activities at a small, midwestern college run by his order. I interviewed Brother Paul as a part of a multigenerational study of alcoholic families. In his mid-50s at the time of our interview, Brother Paul told me that he was an alcoholic but that he had not had a drink for over 20 years. When he was in his 30s, he had been hospitalized for a psychiatric evaluation. He was hospitalized because of his unremitting depression and thoughts of suicide. His drinking problem was diagnosed when he was questioned about the quantity and frequency of his drinking. His heavy drinking had escaped notice because, as director of campus activities, he was obliged to be present at all campus social events. Alcohol was often served, and it seemed natural for him to join in. The extent of his drinking became apparent only when he was asked to review his drinking patterns in detail. Brother Paul readily accepted the diagnosis of alcoholism and agreed to enter alcoholism treatment. He completed treatment and has remained abstinent ever since. He told me: "I just didn't know what it was. As soon as they explained what the problem was, I was relieved to be able to do something about it."

Contrast Brother Paul to the client of a colleague of mine, a federal employee in his early 30s:

Henry initially entered therapy complaining of depression and anxiety following the breakup of a relationship with a woman he had been involved with for five years. Evidence that Henry had a drinking problem was steadily accumulating. He had been arrested several times for drunken driving and, most recently, had gotten so drunk and behaved so badly at a party that his new girlfriend broke up with him. He was stopped by a policeman and charged with drunken driving on the way home from the party, and confessed to my colleague that he didn't remember driving home. At this point, my colleague had him complete a simple checklist that she uses to screen clients for alcohol and drug problems.[1] He checked a number of answers suggestive of alcoholism and she shared this information with him. His response was that alcohol was not a problem to him and he has continued to maintain that position for the past several months, fortifying it with the assertion that his friends all drink as much as he does, or more, but that they're not alcoholics, so he must not be, either. Besides, he maintains, his arrests for drunken driving have occurred over a three-year period of time. One arrest a year for drunken driving is not really a problem.

Why was Brother Paul able to acknowledge and accept treatment for his drinking problem while Henry denies his? The process by which individuals come to recognize an addictive pattern is still not fully understood, nor is it possible to predict, on the basis of drinking behavior alone, which individuals will be motivated to change and which will not. Though Henry's drinking caused him many problems, perhaps Brother Paul was experiencing more pain as a result of his alcoholism. Once he realized that his depression was connected to his drinking, he was willing to give up drinking in order to cure his depression. It may also be possible that Brother Paul's uncontrolled drinking conflicted with his religious principles or that he was simply a more compliant individual.

STAGES OF CHANGE

James Prochaska and Carlo DiClemente have reviewed the literature from a number of fields to isolate stages of change that are common to all addictive processes. For them, recovery from an alcohol or drug problem is much like recovery from any other undesirable habit. It is a matter of unlearning habits and associations that support the addictive habit and learning new habits and associations that promote freedom from the addiction. The stages involved in recovery from alcoholism or drug addiction are much like the stages in recovery from smoking, overeating, or any other undesirable habit.

Stages of Change
(Prochaska and DiClemente)

1. Precontemplation
2. Contemplation
3. Action
4. Maintenance

Precontemplation is the stage that describes Henry. The precontemplative individual is not considering change. In therapy, such clients resist the therapist's efforts to precipitate change. They tend to minimize or deny the negative aspects of their addictive behavior and are not open to such consciousness-raising interventions as observations, confrontation, or interpretation. Substance abuse treatment professionals often use the term "denial" to describe the mechanisms used by such individuals to avoid acknowledging the problematic nature of their addiction.

Clients in the next stage, contemplation, are more receptive to interventions designed to motivate change. Such clients may accept or seek out information about their problem and may be engaged in reevaluating the effects of their addictive behavior and assessing their resources for change. At this stage they may be sensitive to conflicts between their addictive behavior and their values for themselves and their lives.

During the next stage, clients are ready to take action to change their addictive pattern. Prochaska and DiClemente stress that individuals in this stage of change need to feel empowered to carry out the change they visualize. These authors refer to this as a sense of "self-liberation," or the belief that one has the ability to change one's life in key ways. A helping relationship can also be of critical importance at this time in providing motivation and support, but the helping professional should aid the client in recognizing inner resources for change as well.

Maintenance is the final stage in Prochaska and DiClemente's model. It refers to the client's ability to avoid relapse. Maintenance involves learning strategies for coping with stress and temptation without resorting to alcohol or drugs, and maintaining an awareness of the positive benefits of one's new life style.

Prochaska and DiClemente point out that most individuals do not move through these stages in a linear fashion. Their path may be more cyclic. For example, studies of chemically dependent individuals and smokers have shown that the majority of addicted individuals relapse within a year of treatment. However, most individuals who relapse move back to Stage 2 (Contemplation) and eventually try again. Smokers, on average, go through these stages three times before they finally manage to achieve long-term freedom from smoking. Some individuals may get permanently stuck in a particular stage. Prochaska and DiClemente found that, among individuals contemplating quitting smoking, nearly 1/3 were still in the contemplation stage after two years.

Prochaska and DiClemente ask the following question: What are the processes that tend to move individuals along from one stage of change to another? First, they believe that the helping professional is most able to help a client when both are focusing on the same stage of change. Certain change processes are particularly helpful in moving clients at each stage. Clients in the contemplation stage, for example, may be open to information about the negative effects of their drinking or drug use on their health or relationships. Self-reevaluation can help these clients assess their values and modify their self-concept to facilitate change. They may begin to experiment with an image of themselves as a non-drinker. During the action stage, it is important to help clients maintain confidence in their ability to change.

Maintenance involves an open assessment of what situations might encourage relapse and a willingness to plan strategies for coping with such situations. Self-esteem is important as a foundation for maintaining change. Control over stimuli that act as triggers to relapse and over rewards for abstinence are also important in the maintenance stage.

Many techniques for facilitating this stage of recovery are based on the work of Marlatt (1985), who stresses identifying events or experiences that trigger the craving to drink and altering one's response to these triggers.

Prochaska and DiClemente feel that the change processes they identify seem least helpful in the precontemplation period. Exactly what initially motivates individuals to consider the possibility of change is still somewhat mysterious. Prochaska and DiClemente suggest that developmental events may play an important role (for example, turning 40, or having a child). External events may also play a role. For example, a spouse or employer may insist that the individual stop drinking. An individual may be required to enter treatment after an accident or a conviction of driving while intoxicated. Whatever breaks down an individual's denial concerning the negative effects of his addiction contributes to change during this period. Alcoholics Anonymous refers to the process of "hitting bottom," in which an individual is forced to acknowledge that he has lost control of his drinking and of the problems it causes. Employment-based interventions and family confrontations are techniques that are sometimes employed to accelerate the process of hitting bottom. They have sometimes been referred to as techniques for "bringing the bottom up to hit the individual."

Stephanie Brown (1985), Director of the Stanford Alcohol Clinic at Stanford University, studied 80 recovering alcoholics (40 men and 40 women) all of whom had been involved in Alcoholics Anonymous, attempting to understand recovery in terms of cognitive and psychodynamic developmental processes.

Brown examines in detail some of the processes that help precipitate a willingness to change in the alcohol-dependent individual. Her research has identified stages of recovery that are similar in many respects to those of Prochaska and DiClemente. Brown's model is more comprehensive, however, in that she relates changes in the addictive behavior to broader cognitive and affective changes that occur at each stage of recovery. Because her perspective relies very heavily on the cognitive-developmental theory of Jean Piaget, some of Piaget's concepts will be reviewed before her model is presented (see Appendix B for more detail).

COGNITIVE-DEVELOPMENTAL THEORY

Piaget distinguished two main processes by which thought develops. He called them "assimilation" and "accommodation." Assimilation involves understanding or solving a problem using a cognitive tool we already possess: assimilating the situation confronting us to the cognitive structures or "schemes" that we have developed through previous successful problem-solving experiences. A scheme may be a habitual way of understanding or perceiving things, a strategy that has worked for us in the past, or a belief about how things ought to be. Accommodation involves changing some of our thinking in order to cope more effectively with a problem that has presented itself: adapting existing cognitive structures or developing new schemes responsive to the unique features of the new situation. "Assimilation" corresponds roughly to the concept of habit, while "accommodation" relates to learning, although this distinction does not strictly apply. For example, expanding the range of experiences to which I can apply a particular concept is a form of assimilation, but also involves learning.

Assimilation allows us to maximize the benefits of past learning but it can also interfere with our ability to understand new situations. David Reynolds, a therapist and author, quotes a story that illustrates this principle (1989). A young man from India, who had always brewed his tea from loose tea leaves, was given a teabag by his American host. The Indian guest started to tear the bag open to pour the tea leaves into his cup, but was stopped by his host, who explained that, in America, we drop the whole teabag into our cup. The young man complied, then, eager to do the right thing, picked up a packet of sugar and also dropped the packet, unopened, into his cup.

Brown describes denial as a form of "assimilation." In denial, an existing cognitive scheme is stubbornly maintained even when contradicted by reality. For the alcoholic, an important cognitive construct to which reality must be assimilated is the notion "I am not an alcoholic, I am in control of my drinking." Contradictory information is ignored or distorted by the alcoholic so that this conviction can be maintained. In areas that bear on drinking, the alcoholic's thinking may seem quite illogical and rigid, perhaps even childish, due to reliance on assimilation. In areas unrelated to the drinking, however, new information is not as threatening. In these areas, the alcoholic's thinking may be more flexible and differentiated — more mature.

Accommodation occurs when an individual confronts an experience that cannot be understood or mastered using old concepts. This creates a state of conflict or dissonance that forces the individual to learn or create new concepts. For the alcoholic, according to Brown, accommodation occurs when the information challenging the alcoholic's view of reality is so overwhelming that it can no longer be disregarded. The individual is forced to acknowledge that drinking has become a problem. Reporting on her study of recovering alcoholics, Brown found that such an experience often preceded the decision to become involved in Alcoholics Anonymous. This might occur because an individual faced the loss of a job or legal action of some kind due to behavior related to drinking. Medical problems related to drinking might also produce accommodation. Family interventions, in which a number of family members, with the guidance of an experienced professional, unite to confront the alcoholic with evidence about the harm that has resulted from her drinking, can be an effective intervention in overwhelming the alcoholic's denial.

Piaget stresses that human intelligence involves both assimilation and accommodation. We function at our best when assimilation and accommodation are in equilibrium, meaning that we are able both to draw on past experience and to respond to changed circumstances with new ways of thinking. The phenomenon of denial illustrates a state of disequilibrium, in which assimilation prevails over accommodation. Too much accommodation also creates disequilibrium. It is not practical to continually "reinvent the wheel."

Inherent in Piaget's framework is the conviction that learning occurs only when we are confronted with situations that cannot be mastered using the cognitive structures we already possess. Such situations require accommodation, or learning. Learning could not take place, however, if we were not able to combine new ideas with old knowledge to forge new solutions as demanded by the situation.

Piaget distinguished three major modes of thought: sensory-motor, concrete operations, and formal operations. Sensory-motor thought characterizes the infant in the first few years of life. After a transitional period, often called "pre-operational," which lasts roughly until the child begins school, the child enters the period of concrete operations. This stage lasts until adolescence, when formal operations become possible.

Cognitive development, for Piaget, is a process through which an individual's thinking is progressively freed from dependence upon the immediate concrete situation in which the individual finds himself eventually making. The infant in the sensory-motor period forms judgments exclusively on the basis of how his actions affect objects and people with which he comes into contact. The pre-operational toddler and young child recognize that objects and people exist independently of them but they think and act on the basis of the most obvious and striking perceptual cues given off by their environment and can, therefore, be easily misled by superficial appearances. The school-aged child can reason out situations mentally and is less dependent on how things appear, but these mental operations deal only with concrete reality. The adolescent or adult, capable of formal operations, can reason out answers to problems that have no concrete referent, thinking logically, hypothetically, or probabilistically.

At any particular stage in development, an individual will have a characteristic mode of thinking. Not all of her thinking takes place at this level, however. She may respond to some situations with thinking characteristic of an earlier level. Sometimes she may approach problems with thinking typical of a higher developmental level. In studying children's thought, Piaget would characterize children's thinking in terms of the children's modal, or most frequently used, level of thinking, recognizing that they were often capable of solving problems at a somewhat higher level and, at the same time, were sometimes unable to solve problems appropriate for their level.

Individuals vary in how quickly they progress through cognitive stages, and not all individuals reach the higher stages. Presenting individuals with problems that challenge their current level of thinking can encourage learning, but learning depends on physiological maturation as well. Cognitive development can only be accelerated up to a point and may be limited by constitutional factors or organic brain damage. Alcohol and drug abuse, and withdrawal from these substances, may also affect cognitive functioning.

COGNITIVE-DEVELOPMENTAL PSYCHOPATHOLOGY

Brown also draws on the work of Rosen (1985), who has reviewed the literature on what he terms "cognitive-developmental psychopathology," or the use of cognitive developmental principles to understand psychological problems or conditions. In contrast to psychodynamic theorists, who conceive of fixation and regression in affective terms, Rosen is concerned with arrested cognitive functioning. He lists four types of problems in cognitive development that may be present to a greater or lesser degree in various psychopathological conditions. These are:

1. Excessive predominance of assimilation over accommodation, or of accommodation over assimilation.
2. A failure to overcome the egocentric perspective of infancy and early childhood and a consequent inability to distinguish between subject and object or to perceive more than one perspective.
3. Developmental arrest in a particular cognitive stage.
4. Persistence of unrealistic and magical thinking appropriate to the pre-operational period.

According to Brown, these developmental problems are all potential correlates of substance abuse and may affect both the chemically dependent individual and others in the family system.

COGNITIVE-DEVELOPMENTAL STAGES IN RECOVERY

The stages in recovery identified by Brown are: drinking, transition, early recovery, and maintenance. She uses Piaget's concepts of assimilation and accommodation to explain some of the cognitive processes that occur during drinking and recovery, stressing that cognitive factors are very important both in maintaining addictive patterns and in facilitating recovery. The individual who is drinking alcoholically and denying the negative consequences of drinking may demonstrate attributes of pre-operational thought: egocentrism, magical thinking, illogical reasoning, and a focus on irrelevant aspects of a situation. Cognitive functioning during drinking and in early recovery is relatively concrete and relies heavily on assimilation. Later in recovery, an individual can think more abstractly and can process new or complex information more readily. She also uses the concept of "ego flexibility." Ego flexibility refers to the ego's ability to experience a broad range of thoughts, wishes, and feelings. A flexible ego can tolerate and accommodate to a variety of ideas and feelings through using relatively sophisticated defenses and coping strategies. The ego of an individual who is drinking or in early recovery is relatively inflexible. In most cases, ego flexibility increases with recovery. Brown describes her developmental stages as follows.

Drinking

The drinking stage is characterized by denial that drinking is a problem. Denial, in Piagetian terms, involves the predominance of assimilation over accommodation. The cognitive structures that maintain addiction involve denying that there has been a loss of control over drinking and reinforcing the individual's identity as a non-alcoholic, e.g., "I am not an alcoholic, I can control my drinking." Maintaining this belief structure involves a massive constriction of incoming information, to the extent that, where the issue of drinking is concerned, the alcoholic's thinking is illogical and disordered:

> Denial, a primitive defense, requires the systematic exclusion or distortion of environmental data, resulting in a narrow range of what can be assimilated. Drinking individuals who may be capable of more mature cognitive organization in other arenas in which denial is not threatened, or, who operated at a high cognitive level of development before becoming alcoholic, now appear anchored at a level of primitive cognitive development corresponding to the pre-operational phase outlined by Piaget. This level of thinking is concrete. (Brown, 1985)

The illogical and sometimes magical properties of the thinking of alcoholics who refuse to admit that their drinking has become a problem have been responsible for producing countless anecdotes. The retelling of these anecdotes accounts for much of the laughter that characterizes meetings of Alcoholics Anonymous.

> A woman alcoholic remembers her doctor telling her that the particular liver ailment she suffered from was caused by heavy drinking or, in certain rare cases, by eating too many clams. She says she immediately stopped eating clams.

> A man in his late 20s appeared in court, drunk, for a hearing to determine the custody of his stepchildren. The children's mother (his present wife) was in the hospital being treated for bipolar disorder. The children had been staying with their biological father but had been removed because the father had sexually abused them. The stepfather was beginning to go to AA meetings but had not stopped drinking. The judge said to the children's stepfather, who was standing before him weaving from one side to another and visibly intoxicated, "We understand that there is a problem with your drinking that puts the children at risk if placed with you." Continuing to weave precariously from one side to the other in front of the judge, the stepfather replied, much to the amusement of everyone in the courtroom: "Why, there's no problem with my drinking. I'm as sober as . . . as . . . a judge."

Bepko and Krestan (1985) have said, "Treatment in presobriety is the treatment of denial." Denial can be approached directly, through interpretation, confrontation, or the provision of information. It can also be approached indirectly, or strategically. One indirect technique is to accept the client's assertion that she is not an alcoholic and to contract for a certain drinking level. One may take the approach that drinking seems to be causing a problem and, since the person is not an alcoholic, it should be relatively easy to stick to a contract concerning how many drinks will be consumed each day. The person will either stick to the contract (in which case drinking is no longer a problem) or will exceed the contract (in which case she has to admit that she cannot control her drinking). Along similar lines, the therapist may accept the client's unwillingness to quit drinking and, in fact, support it, while continuing to point out the consequences of the drinking. As Bepko and Krestan put it:

> The clinician should continue to convey information about alcoholism at the same time that he restrains the . . . drinker from making hasty decisions or moving into action too quickly. Whenever the client tries to work on other issues, however, the clinician may talk about working toward a dead end, since the drinking will always interfere. (1985, p. 102)

A divorced mother had entered family therapy with her two children, a six-year-old boy and a seven-year-old girl, because her son had behavior problems in school. After several sessions, she confessed to the therapist that she had difficulty implementing his suggestions concerning setting and enforcing limits for her son because she was usually quite drunk in the evening and often could not remember what limits she had set or what consequences she was supposed to initiate. Further questioning made it clear that she became so intoxicated each evening that she passed out on the couch, often leaving her children to put themselves to bed. She was not willing at that time, however, to attend an AA meeting and insisted that she could keep her drinking within manageable limits in the future. The therapist accepted this but continued to point out the connection between her drinking and her failure to set limits each time she described a problem situation where this occurred. He also commented on her inability to keep her drinking within the limits she had chosen. After several months she began attending AA meetings and stopped drinking.

The Transition Phase

In this stage, there is a shift in the individual's core identity from belief that he can control his drinking to an acceptance of loss of control and a new identity as an alcoholic. This new identity is structured at a rather primitive developmental/cognitive level, however, and learning takes place in developmentally primitive ways. Individuals imitate concrete behaviors of individuals they identify with in Alcoholics Anonymous, for example. They learn AA slogans and may identify strongly with their sponsors. Their thinking may be very concrete and they may be able to tolerate only a narrow range of affect. They are easily confused by conflicting expectations and have difficulty coping with situations for which they do not have explicit instructions. Alcoholics Anonymous meetings provide a storehouse of information on specific coping techniques for newly abstinent individuals. Holidays and special family occasions often are one of the first of such crises confronted by the recovering individual. Should one go to a family wedding or Thanksgiving dinner where others are drinking? If so, what should one say when refusing a drink? Whether and how to associate with old drinking or drugging buddies is another frequently encountered problem in early sobriety. Another problem is drinking occasions at work: a birthday or going-away party or a departmental wine-and-cheese party.

Individuals at this point in recovery need practical information and tips on how to resist the temptation to drink and how to cope with situations in which drinking is an issue. They also need reassurance that their recovery is a priority and that they may avoid situations that make them uncomfortable.

Helen, an economist in her mid-40s, who was recovering from an addiction to both alcohol and a variety of mood-altering drugs, attended a professional conference in another city during her second month of recovery. When she registered for her hotel room, she was given a room key and a key to the room's stocked liquor cabinet. "Just drink whatever you like," the clerk told her, "and we'll put it on your bill." Helen panicked at the thought of spending two nights in a room stocked with liquor. She was frightened even to enter the room. In tears, she called her sponsor long distance from the lobby of the hotel. Her sponsor suggested that she return the key to the liquor cabinet to the desk before entering the room and that she attend an AA meeting that evening. Helen followed her sponsor's suggestion and enjoyed the conference.

The Early Recovery Phase

This phase is a more stable continuation of the transitional phase. A new logical structure is developed and differentiated. Individuals involved with AA typically develop a story that lends meaning to their addiction and recovery and acquire a base of experience that helps them to begin making some of their own decisions when they confront new situations. They may re-experience temptation, especially as they branch out from AA in their activities, but they learn to substitute non-alcoholic social patterns for alcoholic ones.

There may be a rather dramatic emergence of affect during this time as experiences from the past are remembered or reinterpreted and as the individual confronts the losses involved in their addiction and recovery. These feelings may threaten the individual's new ego adaptation and sobriety. Depression was frequent in the group Brown studied, occurring in about 2/3 of the individuals during the first year. Also frequent were anxiety and phobias, confusion, and extremes of emotionality. Feelings must be integrated with a cognitive structure supporting abstinence and with the individual's new personal identity.

Because recovery begins with an entirely new cognitive organization, the newly abstinent individual can be thought of as being in an early developmental phase. He or she is at a correspondingly primitive level of cognitive and affective development:

> The defenses and secondary process abstract reasoning that supported denial of alcoholism will not fit the new structure. The individual who appeared to operate at a higher cognitive and affective level during drinking now appears to have lost these abilities or regressed. (Brown, 1985, p. 58)

The individual may frequently feel confused because:

> The cognitive and affective structures based on the new epistemology are too new and undeveloped to integrate environmental stimuli; particularly if that stimulus is unsympathetic to the new belief structure and accompanying behaviors and, instead, emphasizes the old belief structure. (Brown, 1985, p. 57)

An individual in this stage may have great difficulty resolving conflicting information and advice. For example, when an individual in this stage receives one recommendation from her AA sponsor and another, seemingly contradictory, recommendation from her therapist, she may be at a loss as to how to cope. Typically, an individual in early recovery is very literal and concrete in her thinking and in her application of AA principles.

Ongoing Recovery Phase

By this time, behaviors involved in abstinence have become more routine and may feel comfortable or natural to many. The new language and behaviors are well established along with a new identity. The individual's ego flexibility has increased considerably. Cognitively, the individual is operating at a more abstract level and can assimilate new information without major accommodations.

Recovery and sobriety are now not as dependent on the rigidity of certain behaviors or attitudes and the individual is not as dependent upon identification or role models — much has been internalized. The individual has acquired a self-regulating internal structure for sobriety and can tolerate more anxiety than before, using higher level defense mechanisms that permit more self-exploration.

A female client with three years of sobriety decided to renew her commitment to AA and resume attending meetings regularly. She had used AA extensively in early recovery but, in the past few years had stopped attending meetings. She had decided to recommit herself to the program because a recent divorce had caused her to feel more vulnerable to the temptation to drink. As a part of her new regimen, she decided to get a sponsor (she had never had a sponsor when she first joined AA). The woman she asked to be her sponsor was older than she was, and was very motherly and very active in AA. She had only one year of sobriety, however, and differences between the two women soon became apparent. The sponsor was very rigid and literal in her interpretation of the principles of AA while the client, who had experienced a longer period of recovery, was far more flexible. The client eventually terminated the sponsor relationship.

In terms of cognitive development in sobriety, some recovering alcoholics experience cognitive deficits that may limit their ability to go beyond relatively concrete thinking even once they have attained abstinence. Organically-impaired individuals who have difficulty processing abstract information may fail to benefit from those aspects of alcoholism treatment that require clear cognitive functioning and may never attain the cognitive flexibility described by Brown.

> A 19-year-old woman client in inpatient treatment for drug and alcohol problems was frustrated in her attempts to communicate with her father during Family Group sessions. Her father, a recovering alcoholic, had been sober for five years. His thinking was still very concrete, however, and his entire social life revolved around AA meetings. He knew many AA slogans but was not receptive to his daughter's attempts to discuss her feelings about her parents' divorce or her father's abusive treatment of her while her parents were still married. He responded to her attempts to talk about the past by saying only: "I did what I did. I can't blame myself for having a disease."

The chart below summarizes the stages of recovery discussed in this chapter, along with some major goals for intervention at each stage.

Stage	Characteristics	Goals of Intervention
Precontemplation/ Active Addiction	Assimilation, denial	Create conflict or dissonance among cognitive structures
Contemplation/ Transition	Accommodation	Offer new structures
Action/ Early Recovery	Assimilation to new structures	Support and reinforce new structures
Maintenance/ Ongoing Recovery	Equilibrium, "ego flexibility"	Integrate, differentiate, and enlarge structures

During precontemplation, or active addiction, thought is predominantly assimilative, at least in areas of life connected to the addiction. To be effective, an intervention must create some kind of conflict or dissonance among existing cognitive structures. It must pose a problem that the individual is motivated to solve but cannot solve using existing cognitive schemes. In the next stage, contemplation, or transition, the individual has begun to modify cognitive structures, i.e., to accommodate. Effective interventions will offer new structures that support behavior change in the direction of abstinence. In the third stage, action or early recovery, the individual has accepted new ideas and begins to use them to interpret experience. At this stage it is important to reinforce and support the new structures, which are still relatively fragile and inflexible. In later recovery — maintenance, or ongoing recovery — the new structures have been internalized and are used flexibly. Interventions can be aimed at enhancing the complexity and flexibility of these structures to permit the individual greater autonomy and self-awareness.

NOTE

1. There are a number of inventories and checklists that can be used to screen for alcohol and drug problems. One of the simplest of these was devised to assist physicians in detecting alcohol problems in their patients. It is called the CAGE. Its name is a mnemonic to help physicians remember four questions. The questions are: Have you ever felt the need to cut down on alcohol? Do you feel annoyed by people complaining about your drinking? Do you ever feel guilty about your drinking? Do you ever drink eye-openers in the morning? The SMAST (Short Michigan Alcoholism Screening Test) is a good, brief checklist designed to screen for alcohol problems. With minor changes in the wording, it can also be used to screen for drug problems. A copy of the SMAST can be found in Appendix A.

REFERENCES

Bepko, C. and Krestan, J.A. (1985) *The Responsibility Trap.* NY: Free Press.
Brown, S. (1985) *Treating the Alcoholic.* NY: John Wiley & Sons.
Marlatt, G.A. (1985) "Cognitive Factors in the Relapse Process," in *Relapse Prevention: Maintenance Strategies in Addictive Behavior Change,* G.A. Marlatt and J.R. Gordon, eds., NY: Guilford Press.

Prochaska, J.O. and DiClemente, C.C. (1986) "Toward a Comprehensive Model of Change," in *Treating Addictive Behaviors*, W.E. Miller and N. Heather, eds. NY: Plenum.
Reynolds, D.K. (1989) *Pools of Lodging for the Moon*. NY: William Morrow.
Rosen, H. (1985) *Piagetian Dimensions of Clinical Relevance*. NY: Columbia University Press.

Chapter 3

Developmental Trauma and Recovery

Several years ago, I worked with a Family Program in an inpatient alcoholism treatment program for military personnel. One of the patients in that program was a 23-year-old Marine who had referred herself to the program. She had become aware, in the process of participating in a work-site intervention to persuade a colleague to enter treatment, that she herself suffered from all of the symptoms of alcoholism.

When Ellen entered treatment, she described herself as having been extremely promiscuous sexually, beginning at the age of 18, which was also the age when she began drinking heavily. For her, the drinking and the sexual promiscuity had gone hand in hand. She had a severe vaginal infection when she entered treatment, and wanted to be examined for it. Because she was only willing to see a female gynecologist, however, it was several weeks before an appointment could be scheduled for her.

During the week prior to her gynecological exam, she began getting very apprehensive about it. She also remembered during this week, apparently for the first time, that she had been raped at the age of five. This memory elicited a flood of strong feelings about the rape itself and about her adult sexual relationships, many of which had been abusive or, at least, exploitive. It was also followed by tremendously strong feelings of sexual attraction toward other female patients and toward a female nurse, whom the patient particularly admired. These were accompanied by vivid sexual fantasies and dreams involving the nurse and other women. All of this confused and frightened the patient, who emanated an anxiety so strong that it began making other patients in her group, some of whom had sexual abuse histories of their own, anxious. She felt an urge to avoid male patients and was uncomfortable in her patient group, which was predominantly male. Her biggest fear was that this might mean that she was a lesbian, which she felt strongly that she did not want to be.

She was extremely upset and anxious about all of this, but didn't feel she could talk about it in the patient groups or to her male counselors, although she did raise it in the weekly women's group and, on an individual basis, to several of the female counselors, including the occupational therapist.

At first I thought of this as mainly a women's issue. Substance abuse treatment facilities are primarily male environments, not particularly adapted to women's needs. But a few weeks after Ellen's experience, one of the men I interviewed for the Family Program had a similar experience.

One of four brothers, Curt had been raised in a series of foster homes, mostly together with one of his older brothers. In his Family Program interview, he made plans to invite the older brother to participate in the Family Program with him. As family week approached, however, Curt became very apprehensive and admitted in his patient group (for the first time) that he had been sexually abused by his older brother for several years in childhood. After raising the issue in his group he became very upset. He was ashamed of the experiences he had had and fearful that other patients would think he was a homosexual. He was most concerned about his ambivalent feelings about the abuse. He felt frightened and guilty because he had enjoyed some of the experiences. He expressed fear that he would drink if allowed to leave the hospital over the weekend and made a suicide threat that was somewhat half-hearted but which still alarmed the staff.

A female patient left treatment when she became overwhelmed with memories of childhood sexual abuse.

Marta was a 26-year-old Brazilian woman, who worked as a nanny for an American family. Her employer had arranged for her to enter treatment after she had confided to him that she got drunk alone in her room every evening and asked him to find help for her. Marta was a very intelligent woman who had never been able to complete school because she had spent her childhood in Brazil being shuttled from relative to relative, earning her keep through helping with child care and housework. Her mother was young and unmarried and had not been able to take care of her. Marta was very bitter about her childhood. In addition to being deprived of a normal childhood and the opportunity to go to school regularly, she had experienced severe physical abuse in the home in which she had spent the most time, her maternal aunt's. While she discussed this aspect of her background relatively freely, though with much emotion, she alluded to but refused to discuss the sexual abuse that she had experienced in childhood. She said, however, that memories and flashbacks regarding this experience had plagued her since shortly after she entered treatment. She did not feel she could talk about it in her treatment group, which contained only one other woman. She was uncomfortable enough being in such close quarters with so many men as it was. Even apart from the fact that this triggered feelings about the sexual abuse in her past, such closeness between men and women was a culturally unfamiliar experience for Marta, who grew up in a more sex-segregated society. She was also unwilling to discuss it with staff because she feared that once the matter was out in the open, it would come up in the group. In spite of her discomfort with the group, Marta did begin to participate and began to discuss plans for going back to school and completing her education. About halfway through the six-week program, however, Marta left treatment explaining that she didn't feel it was doing her any good because she was not able to talk about the issue she most needed to deal with (the issue of her sexual abuse).

The reactions of Ellen, Curt, and Marta are very similar to those I observed in several Vietnam veterans with post-traumatic stress disorder (PTSD) who participated in a relapse prevention group that I led. This was a group that met weekly to provide the patients with techniques for dealing with the temptation to drink after they left treatment. As the participants told their stories, I was struck by how frequently delayed stress symptoms such as anxiety, phobias, flash-backs, and insomnia had preceded previous relapses in the Vietnam veterans. Research on chemical dependency treatment of Vietnam combat veterans supports the idea that the elimination of alcohol and drugs through chemical dependency treatment may precipitate an exacerbation of stress symptoms in individuals with post-trau-matic stress disorders (Kuhne, Nohner, and Barag, 1986). While this phenomenon is not widely discussed in the literature on sexual abuse survivors or in the literature on chemical dependency treat-ment, it is also true that withdrawal from alcohol or drugs can be the catalyst for a delayed stress reaction in individuals with a sexual abuse history (Courtois, 1988; Bass and Davis, 1988).

DELAYED STRESS REACTIONS TO SEXUAL ABUSE

Delayed stress reactions to early childhood trauma were first de-scribed by Freud and Breuer in their book, published in 1885, enti-tled *Studies on Hysteria* (1966).

Hysteria is a term that was used for a number of years to refer to a cluster of symptoms that seem to have been relatively common among women in the late 1800s and early 1900s. Hysteria is no longer widely used as a diagnostic term, and many of the manifesta-tions of this disorder that were common in Freud's time (such as hysterical paralysis) are relatively rare now. Others have been given their own diagnostic labels (such as "post-traumatic stress disor-der," for example, and "multiple personality disorder," or "anxi-ety disorder").

What Freud and Breuer discovered in their work with this disor-der was that, diverse as the conditions they treated might be, all had a common origin. They all originated in some past psychological trauma: an experience that had called up "distressing affects—such as those of fright, anxiety, shame or physical pain" (Freud and Breuer, 1966). Ideally, unpleasant events are forgotten after awhile, or at least become less distressing. What was distinctive in hysteria was that the psychological trauma seemed to continue to exert an influence on the individual's psychological functioning even though it might have occurred many years before. This was true even though the individual, in a normal state of consciousness, might not remember the event, might not have strong feelings about it, or might not be aware of its significance.

Freud and Breuer asked why events that occurred so long ago continued to exert such a profound influence on certain people. They concluded that the normal reaction to severe psychic trauma is to discharge the unpleasant and intense feelings of fear and help-lessness through action, for example, flight, attack, anger, crying, or screaming. Freud called this "abreaction." Abreaction helps the individual recover from the trauma and move on with life. Some-times, however, trauma occurs under conditions in which the indi-vidual is not allowed to express feelings. Perhaps survival is at stake, and the individual must continue to function calmly and effi-ciently to survive. This may occur in a combat situation, or during a natural disaster such as a flood. Or an individual may be required to ignore her own needs in order to protect or care for another. Freud and Breuer gave the example of an individual caring for a sick fam-ily member. This individual must put the invalid's feelings and needs first, though exposed to many upsetting experiences. Some-times the feelings or the event that provoked them are taboo. Sexual feelings and behaviors, for example, fall into this category. In fact, Freud and Breuer felt that sexual trauma was most often the under-lying cause of the hysteria.

Repression or dissociation, rather than abreaction, may be the most functional responses in such situations. The individual denies to herself what has happened, represses memories of the event, or somehow dissociates herself from the event while still recalling it. But the repressed feelings still have power and find expression through the symptoms that Freud and Breuer observed in their pa-tients. They found that sexual abuse histories were extremely com-monplace among their patients. Many of their patients had been abused by family members, often their fathers. Sexual trauma was particularly difficult to "abreact" and therefore highly likely to produce delayed stress reactions.

Freud argued that when the trauma cannot be abreacted, it is

repressed but continues to exist in the unconscious and continues to
exert an influence. In fact, it pushes for awareness, but there is an
equally strong force (repression) pushing it down into the unconscious. It was this phenomenon that caused Freud to develop the
concept of a "defense." He pointed out that an individual's ego, or
conscious mind, naturally defended itself, through censorship,
against ideas that were incompatible with other consciously held
ideas. Censored ideas, however, did not go away, but persisted in
the unconscious, from which they exerted an influence on the individual's thoughts, feelings, and behavior. Hysterical symptoms
were the symbolic expression of these ideas.

Freud went beyond Breuer's "cathartic method," which relied
on hypnosis to bring the dissociated experience and feelings back to
consciousness, and developed a technique that he called "association" or "free association." Through association, the patient came
closer and closer to the memory of the buried trauma or traumas by
describing associations among intermediary memories or "com-
plexes" of ideas. This technique was the key element in Freud's
method of psychoanalysis, and has continued to prove itself useful
for individuals who are seeking to recover memories of childhood
trauma.

Scholars differ in their explanations for why it occurred, but
agree that even while *Studies on Hysteria* was in the process of
being published, Freud changed his mind about the role of sexual
trauma in the development of emotional disorders as he began to
elaborate on the "drive theory" of development that was described
in Chapter 1. Freud himself said that he simply found it impossible
to believe that so many children had been sexually abused by their
fathers (1977). Eventually Freud came to believe that most of his
patients had only imagined the sexual abuse experiences they reported. In his later writings he talked about children's sexual fantasies concerning their parents but not about parents' sexual feelings
or behavior toward their children. While sympathizing with Freud's
lonely position as the observer of a phenomenon that the medical
profession did not wish to acknowledge, Alice Miller, a contemporary psychoanalytic thinker, has criticized Freud's replacement of
what she calls his "sexual trauma" theory (which places responsi-

bility on the adult) with what she calls his "sexual seduction" theory (which blames the child victim) (1986). She argues that when children experience sexual fantasies about their parents they are usually responding to sexual stimulation or abuse by the parents. She points out that even in the Oedipus story from which the term "Oedipus complex" was taken, Oedipus was the victim of his parents. Attributing sexual desires to children when they have, in fact, been abused by adults, is an example of what she calls "poisonous pedagogy," an approach to child-rearing that assigns guilt for parental wrongs to the child while at the same time insisting that the child be grateful for how he or she has been raised. Parents who raise their children in this manner, according to Miller, are unsympathetic to their children's needs because they themselves were raised by parents who abused them and were insensitive to *their* needs. To acknowledge that they are inflicting pain on their children is impossible because it would involve accepting the pain they experienced as children and admitting that their parents did not protect or validate them adequately.

OTHER DELAYED STRESS RESPONSES

While the mental health profession, influenced by Freud, for many years tended to deny the significance of sexual trauma as a factor in the development of a number of individuals, other kinds of delayed stress reactions were still being observed and treated. Delayed stress responses were observed among combatants in World War I and first described in the literature as "war neurosis" (Freud, 1959). After World War II, similar symptoms were documented in survivors of Nazi persecution and labelled "survivor syndrome" (Berger, 1977; Krystal, 1968). In the 1970s, the emergence among Vietnam combat veterans of delayed stress reactions provided the impetus for efforts to understand the syndrome (Goodwin, 1980) and resulted in the development of a diagnostic category for "post-traumatic stress disorder." The DSM-III-R defines post-traumatic stress disorder as involving:

> The development of characteristic symptoms following a psychologically distressing event that is outside the range of usual human experience . . . . The stressor producing this syndrome would be markedly distressing to almost anyone, and is usually experienced with intense fear, terror, and helplessness. The characteristic symptoms involve re-experiencing the traumatic event, avoidance of stimuli associated with the event or numbing of general responsiveness, and increased arousal. (APA, 1987)

Delayed stress reactions that are less intense than post-traumatic stress disorder as defined in the DSM-III-R or that involve only one or two of the symptoms listed may also occur, either as part of another emotional disorder such as anxiety disorder, somatoform disorder, or dissociative disorder, or in the absence of any diagnosable psychopathology (Courtois, 1988).

In 1973, Horowitz developed a model of the delayed stress response syndrome that he later applied to Vietnam veterans (Horowitz and Solomon, 1975). Horowitz's model incorporated earlier theories of delayed stress reactions, including Freud's, and emphasized the cognitive, or information-processing, aspects of response to stress. This conceptualization has been used more recently to describe delayed stress reactions among sexual abuse victims (Courtois, 1988).

The process of coping cognitively and emotionally with traumatic stress, according to Horowitz, involves four stages:

Stage 1. OUTCRY: Initial realization that the stress has occurred (often with an emotional "outcry").

Stage 2. DENIAL: Denial and numbness.

Stage 3. OSCILLATION: Mixed phase of oscillation between denial with numbness and intrusive repetition in thought, emotional pangs, and/or compulsive/repetitive behaviors.

Stage 4. WORKING THROUGH: Working through and acceptance, with loss of the peremptory quality of either the denial or the recollection of the stress event.

(Adapted from Horowitz, 1973).

Working through means to accept that the event happened, feeling the distressing feelings that accompany this acceptance, and then placing the event into some kind of a cognitive framework that provides a sense of completion or resolution. Working through involves accommodation because new cognitive structures must be evolved to reconcile this previously unthinkable occurrence with the individual's existing cognitive schema. An individual can get stuck in one of the earlier stages of this process. Horowitz's point of view holds that catharsis alone is not sufficient to relieve an individual of the long-term effects of early trauma. Cognitive mastery is also essential. The individual must make some kind of sense of the event, must be able to stand outside the event and have some sort of a perspective on it. To the same extent, cognitive mastery alone is also inadequate. An intellectual understanding is not enough – the individual must also experience the feelings involved.

There are a number of factors influencing whether or not an individual can work through a traumatic event at the time it happens. They include the following: how overwhelming the feelings are; the individual's ability to tolerate anxiety and other unpleasant affect; the degree of sophistication of the ego defenses available to the individual; the extent to which the individual can safely express the feelings involved; the kinds of emotional and social support that are available; the degree to which the individual can be protected from a recurrence of the stressful event; and the individual's level of cognitive functioning.

LONG-TERM EFFECTS OF CHILDHOOD TRAUMA

Children are at a disadvantage where many of the factors listed above are concerned and are particularly vulnerable to dissociative reactions to trauma. Because they are cognitively more immature than adults and often unable to express their feelings in words, they may have more trouble achieving cognitive mastery of traumatic experiences. When sexual or physical abuse is involved, they are frequently afraid to tell anyone they have been abused. They may not be believed, supported, or protected when they do tell. Children, by definition, lack mature emotional and cognitive resources. They do not have sophisticated defenses that allow them to gradually assimilate information; denial may be all they have. Children have a different sense of time than adults and fewer resources for dealing with negative feelings. Children, especially in certain stages of development, may lack the cognitive skills necessary to understand or gain perspective on what has happened.

Abused children, especially when there is no intervention, may have few resources to draw on in terms of completing Horowitz's ideal process of working through the stress produced by a traumatic event. Children who cannot complete the working through process may defend themselves against psychological distress by denying that the event occurred, by avoiding reminders of it, or by numbing their feelings about it. They may eventually learn to use alcohol or drugs to reinforce the process of "denial-numbing" described by Horowitz. Though the individual may not consciously remember the traumatic event or the associated feelings, he or she may symbolically relive the event without being consciously aware of it. For example, an individual sexually abused as a child may become promiscuous and experience further abuse or may abuse others. He or she may be self-destructive, imitating the harm that was done by others. Freud pointed to the existence of a "repetition compulsion" — a need to repeat an upsetting experience in an attempt to master it. He also described a phenomenon called "identification with the aggressor," in which an individual identifies with and imitates the powerful person who has caused him or her harm. This may result in the abuse victim becoming an abuser as an adult.

Even though memories have been repressed, particular events, situations, or developmental changes may trigger unbidden thoughts, images, or memories connected to the event. This may be many years after the event. When an adult has difficulty with a particular developmental task, childhood trauma may be one factor contributing to the difficulty. Life events that recall the original trauma may, on occasion, trigger full blown "intrusive-repetitive" crises: memory flooding, panic or anxiety attacks, sexual identity panics, nightmares, phobias, etc. Sometimes "revictimization" (for example, rape) will trigger an "intrusive-repetitive" episode. Freud and Breuer observed that their patients' hysterical symptoms were often precipitated by an event that later proved to be associated with childhood sexual trauma.

Studies of individuals being treated for substance abuse reveal that many report being sexually abused as children. Rohsenow and colleagues (1988) questioned 398 patients in substance abuse treatment and found that 14 percent of the adult men and 75 percent of the adult women reported that they had been sexually abused as children. The adolescents in treatment, particularly the males, were even more likely to report such experiences — 39 percent of the teenaged boys and 77 percent of the teenaged girls. A substantial proportion of substance abusers have been molested by members of their own family. Benward and Densen-Gerber (1975) found that among 118 women being treated for chemical dependency, 44 percent had had at least one incestuous experience in childhood. Harrison and Lumry (1984) reported that 25 percent of the female substance abusers they studied and 15 percent of the males had experienced incest as children. In a study of 117 alcoholic women, Kovach found that 22 percent had experienced incest as children. Of these women, 40 percent exhibited symptoms of post-traumatic stress disorder (1986). The relative frequency of childhood sexual abuse among substance abusers is not surprising when one considers that a high proportion of substance abusers grew up in homes where at least one parent was dependent on alcohol or drugs and therefore were at higher risk than average for both substance abuse and sexual victimization (Donaldson and Gardner, 1985).

SEXUAL ABUSE ISSUES IN SUBSTANCE ABUSE TREATMENT

Intrusive-repetitive symptoms may be triggered by conditions that resemble or evoke feelings or memories connected to the original experience of sexual abuse. Intrusive-repetitive symptoms may also be triggered by situations in which the individual feels safe and trusting and, therefore, less defended. Substance abuse treatment settings contain a number of potential triggers of both kinds. These are shown in the list below.

Common Triggers for Delayed Stress Reactions to Sexual Abuse in Substance Abuse Treatment

- Withdrawal of Substance/Loss of Ability to Self-Medicate
- Loss of Control
- Apprehensive Waiting
- Medical Context
- Gynecological/Physical Exams
- Intrusive Questioning
- Confrontive Tactics to Break Down Denial
- Proximity to Same Sex
- Proximity to Opposite Sex
- Physical Contact
- Acceptance and Support
- Relationship with Helping Professionals
- ACOA Films/Lectures
- Sharing One's Story
- Hearing Others' Stories

Abstinence from alcohol or drugs alone can weaken a chemically dependent individual's capacity to deny a past sexual abuse experience or can numb the associated emotions, and may be sufficient to produce intrusive-repetitive symptoms. In inpatient settings, an individual experiences a degree of loss of control and may spend a certain amount of time waiting, sometimes apprehensively, for a scheduled event or appointment. These situations may be reminiscent of the original abuse situation (for example, an individual may have waited apprehensively in childhood, to see if the abuser would pass the door to her bedroom or open it). If the child was taken to a hospital or other health care setting after the abuse, then the medical context of an inpatient setting may evoke feelings associated with that experience, especially if the individual receives a gynecological or physical exam as a part of, or prior to, substance abuse treatment. Medical examinations may also trigger memories of the abuse itself or of later examinations or treatment. The questions asked by mental health and substance abuse professionals may seem intrusive to the client and may also evoke either the original abuse experience or feelings about care received following the abuse.

Substance abuse counselors employ a number of confrontive tactics to break down the individual's denial concerning the substance abuse problem. These interventions may also break down denial in other areas such as sexual acting out, sexual revictimization, or the repressed abuse experience itself. When the individual is unaccustomed to being physically close to individuals of the opposite sex, the physical proximity engendered in a treatment situation or in AA or NA meetings may trigger sexual fears or feelings in individuals who have repressed earlier sexual abuse. Physical proximity to individuals of the same sex may have a similar effect in vulnerable individuals. Physical contact (e.g., hugging) is common in treatment settings and in 12-step programs, and may have a similar effect.

The acceptance and support an individual experiences from a therapist or counselor, from peers, or from members of AA or NA may create a sense of safety and trust that enable the individual to experience previously denied memories or feelings. Relationships with helping professionals may evoke preadolescent feelings surrounding authority and dependence that were related to the original abuse experience.

Books, films, and lectures about adult children of alcoholics and characteristics of dysfunctional families are often provided or recommended to individuals in recovery. These may stimulate new memories or new understandings of the past. Telling one's story, either in a treatment group or in 12-step meetings, may also result in new perceptions of one's history. Finally, hearing others' stories, especially when they involve abuse, may trigger memories, identify feelings, or simply raise an individual's awareness about what sexual abuse is, causing them to see their past in a new light.

Individuals in substance abuse treatment who have a post-traumatic stress disorder due to childhood sexual abuse may be "difficult clients" (Cole, 1985). When denial-numbing symptoms predominate, individuals are often anxious and depressed (Kovach, 1986), and may be reluctant to participate in group therapy or self-help groups due to difficulty in trusting others and a tendency to **isolate themselves** (Skorina and Kovach, 1986).

Intrusive-repetitive crises during substance abuse treatment can produce any of the feelings and behaviors listed below.

Common Signs of Post-Traumatic Distress
Following Sexual Abuse

- Anxiety
- Panic Attacks
- Insomnia
- Nightmares
- Vivid Memories and Flashbacks
- Flooding
- Sexual Identity Crises
- "Inappropriate" Sexual Feelings and Behavior
- Other "Inappropriate" Behavior
- Suicide Threats/Attempts
- Other Self-Destructive Behavior

Horowitz's treatment model dictates different interventions for the "denial-numbing" and the "intrusive-repetitive" phases of delayed stress reactions. Interventions most often appropriate in the denial-numbing stage stress helping the patient gain access to the repressed experience in order to process it. These are the techniques additionally used in psychodynamically-oriented psychotherapy. Typical "uncovering" techniques for this phase are summarized below.

Traditional "Uncovering" Interventions

- Reduce Structure
- Reduce Defenses
- Encourage Recall Through
  - Description
  - Association
  - Symbolization
- Explore Emotion
- Encourage Abreaction/"Working Through"

Such interventions are not appropriate early in recovery from alcoholism or drug addiction. They are also not appropriate during an intrusive-repetitive crisis. Some appropriate stabilizing interventions in these circumstances are listed below.

Interventions During Crisis

• Reinforce Substance Abuse Recovery Program
• Provide Emotional Support
• Provide Cognitive Framework
• Normalize Experience
• Encourage Structure
• Identify Triggers
• Assess External Demands
• Assess Social Supports
• Assess Relaxation and Stress Reduction Techniques
• Differentiate "Now" from "Then"

The first order of business is to reinforce the individual's substance abuse program. Without recovery from the substance abuse, recovery from the sexual abuse cannot take place. Within that framework, it is important to provide the client with support and with a cognitive framework that helps her understand the reason for her frightening feelings. It is important to reassure her that she does not have to immediately understand or resolve the issues posed by her memories of the initial trauma, or to give them all of her attention. Some of the client's anxiety can be reduced by providing assurance that the experience, frightening as it may be, is relatively common among recovering individuals and actually represents a healing process.

It can be helpful to encourage the client to maintain a daily structure. The AA philosophy of "One Day at a Time" can be useful in reinforcing this perspective. It is also useful to identify triggers so that the client can avoid them when necessary. For example, many recovering individuals experience a flood of memories and feelings when they begin attending meetings for adult children of alcoholics. These clients may wish to postpone participation in such groups until they have a stable period of long-term recovery.

The helping professional can help the client assess external demands and social supports to assure that they are balanced, manageable, and not negative. Many clients benefit from using relaxation and stress reduction techniques, but, again, these must be assessed in light of each client's unique situation to determine whether they are helpful or whether they act as further triggers. Massage, for example, is relaxing to some clients but may trigger upsetting body memories in others. Finally, it is important to help the client differentiate past from present and to remind the client that the abuse happened in the past.

"RESILIENT CHILDREN," OR "SURVIVORS"

Just because an individual has experienced childhood sexual abuse and has used alcohol or drugs to facilitate denial of memories or feelings does not mean that that individual is in any way permanently damaged. Recovery from both sexual abuse and substance abuse can be rapid and dramatic.

In addition, many abused children do grow up without serious mental health problems. It appears that some individuals may have social supports, psychological characteristics, or coping skills that give them a special resilience or ability to survive in adverse situations.

Comparisons between individuals with an abuse history who have sought help for psychological problems and those with an abuse history who have not sought such assistance can be informative. If one makes the assumption that individuals who have not sought such help have been better able to cope with the abuse they experienced, then comparing the two populations can provide clues as to what factors promote coping with early abuse. Such research suggests that while childhood trauma can be damaging, there are also protective factors that can promote normal development in abused children. These include: intelligence and cognitive maturity; ego-strength; coping skills; stability of environment; family support; other social support; positive school experiences; a sense of "efficacy," or of having chosen responses to events that occurred; and the ability to place the traumatic events into some kind of cognitive framework, or to feel that they somehow make sense (Conte and Schuerman, 1987; Courtois, 1988; Tsai, Feldman-Summers, and Edgar,1979; Lynch and Roberts, 1982; Rutter, 1981).

Mrazek and Mrazek (1987), two therapists who have done a great deal of work with children, have listed the coping skills that they think are particularly important in enabling children to survive adverse situations. They are: rapid responsivity to danger, or hypervigilence; precocious maturity; dissociation of affect; information seeking; formation and utilization of relationships for survival; positive fantasies about the future; decisive risk taking; the conviction of being loved (whether or not it is true); idealization of an aggressor's competence (which, perversely, can raise self-esteem through "identification with the aggressor"); cognitive restructuring of painful experiences to cast them in a more positive light; altruism (because the individual may experience positive social experiences and a sense of worth through helping others, such as younger siblings); and optimism and hope.

It is interesting that many of these coping skills are ones we tend to see as symptoms when they manifest themselves as personality traits. Hypervigilence, dissociation, precociousness, manipulativeness, and identification with an abusive parent, for example, may have a positive effect in buffering children from harm, but these and other protective factors may be dysfunctional if they become a major part of the child's behavioral repertoire and are still relied on heavily even after the child is no longer in the harmful situation.

It can be helpful in the therapeutic situation to be aware of the fact that these behaviors were, initially, positive and adaptive responses to the situation in which the individual found himself. Even the response of using alcohol or drugs to self-medicate against post-traumatic distress symptoms can be seen as a resourceful one, under the circumstances. Making this clear to the individual, while supporting change, can help enhance the individual's sense of competence and self-worth.

REFERENCES

American Psychiatric Association (APA) (1987) *Diagnostic and Statistical Manual of Mental Disorders* (3rd Edition Revised). Washington, DC: American Psychiatric Association.

Bass, E. and Davis, L. (1988) *The Courage to Heal*. NY: Harper & Row.

Benward, J. and Densen-Gerber, J. (1975) "Incest as a Causative Factor in Anti-Social Behavior. An Exploratory Study," *Contemporary Drug Problems, 4*, 3: 323-340.

Berger, D.M. "The Survivor Syndrome: A Problem of Nosology and Treatment." *American Journal of Psychotherapy*, v. 31, no. 2, 1977, 238-251.

Cole, C.L. (1985) "A Group Design for Adult Female Survivors of Childhood Incest." *Women and Therapy, 4*, 3: 71-82.

Conte, J.R. and Schuerman, J.R. (1987) "Factors Associated with an Increased Impact of Child Sexual Abuse," *Child Abuse and Neglect*, v. 11, 201-211.

Courtois, C.A. (1988) *Healing the Incest Wound*. NY: W.W. Norton.

Donaldson, M.A. and Gardner, R. (1985) "Diagnosis and Treatment of Traumatic Stress among Women after Childhood Incest," in *Trauma and Its Wake*, C.R. Figley, ed., 356-377. NY: Brunner/Mazel.

Freud, S. (1959) "Psychoanalysis and War Neurosis." In *Collected Papers*. v. 5. NY: Basic Books.

Freud, S. (1977) *Five Lectures on Psychoanalysis*. NY: W.W. Norton.

Freud, S. and Breuer, J. (1966) *Studies on Hysteria*. NY: Avon Books.

Goodwin, J. (1980) "The Etiology of Combat-Related Post-Traumatic Stress Disorders," in *Post-Traumatic Stress Disorders of the Vietnam Veteran*, T. Williams, ed., 1-23. Cincinnati: Disabled American Veterans.

Harrison, P.A. and Lumry, A.E. (1974) "Female Sexual Abuse Victims: Perspectives on Family Dysfunction, Substance Use and Psychiatric Disorders." Paper presented at the Second National Conference for Family Violence Researchers, University of New Hampshire, Durham, NH.

Horowitz, M.J. (1973) "Phase Oriented Treatment of Stress Response Syndrome," *American Journal of Psychotherapy*, v. 27, no. 4, 1973, 506-515.

Horowitz, M.J. and Solomon, G.F. (1975) "A Prediction of Delayed Stress Response Syndrome in Vietnam Veterans," *Journal of Social Issues*, v. 31, 67-80.

Horowitz, M.J. (1986) *Stress Response Syndromes*. (Second Edition.) Northvale, NJ: Jason Aronson, Inc.

Kovach, J.A. (1986) "Incest as a Treatment Issue for Alcoholic Women," *Alcoholism Treatment Quarterly*, 3, 1: 1-13.

Krystal, H. (1968) *Massive Psychic Trauma*. NY: International Universities Press.

Kuhne, A., Nohner, W., and Barag, G. (1986) "Efficacy of Chemical Dependency Treatment as a Function of Combat in Vietnam," *Journal of Substance Abuse Treatment*, 3: 191-194.

Lynch, M.A. and Roberts, J. (1982) *Consequences of Child Abuse*. London: Academic Press.

Miller, A. (1986) *Thou Shalt Not Be Aware*. NY: Meridian Books.

Mrazek, P.J. and Mrazek, D.A. (1987) "Resilience in Child Maltreatment Victims: A Conceptual Exploration," *Child Abuse and Neglect*, v. 11, 357-366.

Rohsenow, D., Corbett, H.B., and Devine, D. (1988) "Molested as Children: A Hidden Contribution to Substance Abuse," *Journal of Substance Abuse Treatment*, v. 5, 13-18.

Rutter, M. (1981) "Resilient Children" *Psychology Today*, September, 57-66.

Skorina, J.K. and Kovach, J.A. (1986) "Treatment Techniques for Incest-Related Issues in Alcoholic Women," *Alcoholism Treatment Quarterly*, 3, 1: 17-30.

Tsai, M., Feldman-Summers, S., and Edgar, M. (1979) "Childhood Molestation: Variables Related to Differential Impacts on Psychosexual Functioning in Adult Women," *Journal of Abnormal Psychology*, 88, 407-417.

Chapter 4

Family Recovery
As a Developmental Process

An earlier chapter described the Cutters, a couple who had, as yet, been unable to complete the task of developing a pattern for sharing parental responsibilities. Sandra, the wife, had assumed full responsibility for parenting the children while her husband, Jim, whose work kept him away from home most of the time, continued to live a bachelor life involving women, parties, and drugs. It is not unusual for families in which substance abuse is a problem to have difficulty negotiating family developmental tasks.

Like individuals, families have developmental stages and developmental tasks. The following chart shows the stages a family is commonly expected to go through in our society. Divorce has also been portrayed because it is frequent, even though it is not generally expected. Remarriage also consists of a series of stages, though this and other variations on the family life cycle are not depicted in the chart.

Typical Stages in Family Life Cycle

Life Cycle Stages	Key Tasks
EXPECTED STAGES:	
Leaving home: single young adults	Accepting emotional and financial responsibility for self
The joining of families through marriage	Commitment to new system

Life Cycle Stages	Key Tasks
Families with young children	Accepting new members into system
Families with adolescents	Increasing flexibility of family boundaries to include children's independence and grandparents' frailties
Launching children and moving on	Accepting a multitude of exits from and entries into the family system
Families in later life	Accepting the shifting of generational roles

COMMON VARIATION:

Divorce

The decision to divorce	Acceptance of inability to resolve marital tension sufficiently to continue relationship
Planning the breakup of the system	Supporting viable arrangements for all parts of the system
Separation	a. Willingness to continue cooperative coparental relationship and joint financial support of children b. Work on resolution of attachment to spouse
The divorce	More work on emotional divorce: overcoming hurt, anger, guilt, etc.

Post-divorce family

Single-parent custodial	Willingness to maintain financial responsibilities, continue parental contact with ex-spouse and support contact of children with ex-spouse and his or her family

Life Cycle Stages	Key Tasks
Single-parent non-custodial	Willingness to maintain parental contact with ex-spouse and support custodial parent's relationship with children

(Adapted from Carter and McGoldrick, 1980)

As it moves through the life cycle, a family must complete each developmental task as a unit, moving from one life cycle stage to the next. It must also facilitate each individual family member's development and help each individual move from one developmental stage to the next as appropriate.

Transition points in the family life cycle and transitions for individual family members are stressful for families. Family systems theorists explain this by pointing out that family systems seek homeostasis, or stability, in the relationships among various parts of the system. Change upsets the family system's equilibrium. When this occurs, family members will seek to restore equilibrium. Accommodation (in Piaget's sense) is one way of restoring equilibrium. The family strives to create a new equilibrium that incorporates the changed elements of the situation. Faced with a teenager who challenges family rules and boundaries, for example, parents may choose to accept greater independence from their child in some areas, while remaining firm in others. The family system is restabilized with some changes. Change is an inevitable aspect of family life. Members are always growing older and moving from one life cycle stage to another; family composition changes over time as individuals are born, die, leave home, marry, or divorce. Maintaining stability in the face of change is an ongoing issue for all families. In family systems where substance abuse is a problem, family homeostasis may depend on that substance. The recovery of the chemically dependent individual, though a positive development for the family, may threaten the stability of the family system and thus provoke anxiety in family members.

FAMILY SYSTEMS APPROACHES
TO SUBSTANCE ABUSE

Family systems theory developed out of attempts to explain how families preserve their identity, structure, and cohesiveness as they experience the changes that inevitably accompany family life. Much of the original work in family systems theory resulted from attempts of clinicians and researchers to understand families of schizophrenics. Many of these families seemed to maintain too much stability in the face of change. For example, when the schizophrenic family member returned home after a hospitalization, these families were unable to make the kinds of changes that clinicians working with the schizophrenic family member felt would support compensatory functioning in the schizophrenic. The schizophrenic often seemed to lose ground upon returning home.

It is still not clear the extent to which the family patterns in these schizophrenic families differed from those typical of any families with a chronically ill member. At the time, those who studied these families agreed that the families often relied on unusually rigid perceptions and family rules to maintain homeostasis, or to defend the family against conflict or disequilibrium. Often these patterns could be maintained only through denying or distorting reality (see, e.g., Lidz et al., 1957; Wynne et al., 1958), including the inner reality of individual family members. It was felt that tendencies on the part of the family to distort or deny feelings and facts made it difficult for the schizophrenic to maintain a grasp on reality. Gregory Bateson and his colleagues (1956) used the term "double bind" to refer to the kinds of paradoxical statements and demands family members appeared to make. These double binds were thought to represent an attempt to deal with underlying conflicts without acknowledging them openly. R.D. Laing took the position that the schizophrenic's unintelligible communications often made sense in the context of the family matrix and that these communications often were relatively truthful statements about family reality (Laing, 1971; Laing and Esterson, 1973). During the early years of family systems theory, such family processes as those described by Bateson and Laing were thought to have caused the development of the schizophrenia. Now that the role of biochemical factors in the etiology of schizophrenia is being given more weight, less emphasis is placed on the role of family interaction in causing schizophrenia. Family processes are acknowledged to result to a great extent from, or at least to be exacerbated by, the family's attempts to cope with the chronic stresses imposed on them by the schizophrenic member. Stephanie Brown (1988) has reviewed findings from research on families with a physically disabled family member and found that these families also develop a number of defensive maneuvers aimed at maintaining family stability in the face of the disruption caused by the presence of a disabled family member. Once they have become a part of the families' functioning, however, these adaptive processes can reinforce maladaptive behaviors on the part of the schizophrenic. When such patterns are transmitted from one generation to the next, and schizophrenia appears in more than one generation, it can be difficult to separate family functioning that reflects pathology from family functioning that produces pathology.

Salvatore Minuchin, a clinician and family systems theorist who has studied the structural aspects of family systems, formulated many of his ideas in a different context. He spent a large part of his career working with families of delinquent and neglected children and found that many of these families were, in a sense, not rigid enough. Sometimes they lacked clear rules and a workable authority structure (Minuchin, 1984). Rather than being too rigid, they were too chaotic.

Family systems theorists who have studied alcoholism have found both rigidity and chaos in families with an alcoholic member. They have observed that the family system is affected when a member of the family is dependent on alcohol, just as the family system is affected by the presence of a chronically ill, schizophrenic, or disabled family member. As for the other conditions, family patterns and individual problems can be mutually reinforcing. Family processes that evolve to cope with a member's alcoholism may help maintain the alcohol problem. These processes may be transmitted from one generation to the next, so that an individual who grows up in a family with an alcoholic parent may have internalized a conception of family roles that includes behaviors connected to alcoholism. Through "assortive mating" (the tendency to marry someone similar to one's self) they may find themselves married to someone who shares a similar set of expectations. The couple, then, may develop a style of family functioning that transmits these expectations to their children.

Berenson (1976) has used the phrases "wet states" and "dry states" to indicate how alcohol dependence can affect a family system. The term "wet state" refers to how a family system functions when a member is under the influence of alcohol. "Wet state" functioning is usually quite different from family functioning during a "dry state." In some families it may be chaotic or out of control. This may be particularly true for families in which "episodic," or "binge" drinking prevails. During "dry" periods, families may be characterized by rigidity and denial, and by a desperate attempt to maintain control.

Family systems theory holds that alcoholic drinking may have adaptive, as well as disruptive, consequences for a family, especially once the family has begun to organize itself around the drinking. For example, drinking may help, as well as hinder, conflict resolution in families. Theodore Jacob, of the University of Arizona Family Studies Program, has been conducting an intensive and detailed study of family interaction carried out in the homes of families where one parent is an alcoholic, comparing them to normal families and to families in which one parent is depressed. Jacob and his colleague Seilhamer have found that alcoholic drinkers show distinctive patterns of managing conflict when they have been drinking (Jacob and Seilhamer, 1987). Steady drinkers and their wives engaged in more productive problem solving when the alcoholic was drinking than when he was not drinking. Episodic drinkers and their wives engaged in more conflict and less successful problem solving resolution when the alcoholic was drinking than when he was not.

Peter Steinglass and his colleagues (1987) have studied the kinds of rules and rituals that families evolve to cope with oscillation between "wet" and "dry" states. Families may change their patterns to accommodate to a family member's drinking or to prevent the alcoholic's drinking from interfering with family activities. Steinglass tells the story, for example, of a family who, for years, had spent their annual summer vacation at a rather isolated cottage resort on the lake that was a day's drive from their home. Over the years, the father developed a serious drinking problem, spending most days, after work, at the bar. Even at work he was intoxicated most of the time. As his limitations became more apparent, the family became nervous about letting the father drive to the resort and about how he would manage activities such as boating and fishing. They finally decided to change their longstanding summer tradition and began going to a resort near home to preserve their vacation tradition without confronting the father's alcoholism or interfering with his drinking. The fact that the resort was near home meant the mother did not have to rely on the father to drive. Because the resort was in an area known for its bars, the family was able to spend its days at the beach, and the husband spent his days in the bars.

Alterations of family rituals to take into account a family member's drinking can minimize some of the damage that might otherwise be caused by alcoholism and by the family's oscillation between "wet" and "dry" states. They also reflect the inroads on family well-being made by alcoholism. In fact, Steinglass has found that the degree to which family rituals are altered or given up entirely is a good indicator of how severe the alcoholism is and of how adversely it has affected family members. When family rituals are maintained, offspring are less likely to develop alcoholic drinking patterns themselves.

Family roles also are typically adjusted to compensate for alcoholism in a family member, particularly when the alcoholic is one of the parents. Murray Bowen (1978) has used the terms "underfunctioning" and "overfunctioning" to describe how family roles may change when one member is unable to carry out his or her normal responsibilities. Alcoholism typically impairs an individual's ability to carry out family responsibilities. Failure to monitor children's behavior adequately is often a consequence of problem drinking. Other possible areas of "underfunctioning" for the alcoholic include household responsibilities, wage-earning, emotional support of the other spouse, and other aspects of child-rearing. When this occurs, the spouse of an alcoholic often begins to take on more and more of the alcoholic's responsibilities in order to keep the family functioning smoothly. Children, also, may take on tasks that belong to the alcoholic parent or that belong to the non-alcoholic parent, now overburdened with the alcoholic's responsibilities. These family members are "overfunctioning." Substance abuse treatment specialists often refer to "overfunctioning" as "enabling." This is because, in taking on the alcoholic's responsibilities, other family members help the alcoholic avoid the negative consequences that would otherwise result from drinking.

Another term that has become popular in substance abuse treatment is "codependence." Many mental health professionals have negative reactions to the fact that this term is often broadly used to refer to any one of a number of attitudes and behaviors that might otherwise simply be described as "dependence." But the term was initially developed to refer to a quite specific phenomenon. "Codependence," as originally used, referred to the family systems proposition that once one family member is dependent upon a substance, and the family has organized itself around that dependency, all family members become dependent on the substance, or "codependent," because family homeostasis requires its presence. In recent years, the term "codependence" has been detached from its origins and is now used more loosely to refer to a set of personality traits that predispose an individual to chronically "overfunction" in relationships, thus enabling "underfunctioning" in others.

LIFE CYCLE STAGES IN ALCOHOLIC FAMILIES

The effects of alcoholism on the family system may be different at different stages in the family life cycle. For example, drinking that began relatively late in the alcoholic's life may have less effect on the family system than alcoholism that has been present since an earlier point in the family life cycle.

Alcoholism can affect how a family manages its developmental tasks and the extent to which families can support members' completion of their own developmental transitions. Because alcoholic families resist change, life cycle transitions are often difficult for such families. Alcoholic families also have their own developmental stages. Steinglass and his colleagues have described three key stages in the life cycle of alcoholic families.

Early Phase: Establishing Boundaries and Identity

This stage begins when a family member begins to show signs of an alcohol problem. This issue can come up at any point in the family life cycle — as early as during the parent's courtship and as late as old age, perhaps after the death of a spouse. The question to be resolved in this stage is, will the family permit or accommodate to alcoholism in a family member or not? If the family refuses to accept alcoholism in a member, divorce may occur. Or, if the problem drinking becomes apparent during courtship, marriage may never take place. Adult children of alcoholics may fail to notice warning signs of alcoholism in potential mates. They may be predisposed to accommodate to a partner's alcoholism when it becomes apparent. On the other hand, if they have made a conscious attempt to break with the alcoholism in their family of origin, they may refuse to accept it in a partner. The research carried out by Steinglass and his colleagues has shown that adult children from alcoholic families who consciously attempt to develop a new set of rituals and routines that do not support alcoholism are more likely to break with familial alcoholism.

Middle Phase: Commitment and Stability

The question in this stage is, will the family organize itself around a family member's drinking? This has to do with the extent to which the family system adapts to the problem drinking. Such adaptations (e.g., overfunctioning on the part of the spouse) may act as a buffer, protecting the family and its members from negative consequences due to the drinking. At the same time, these adaptations reflect an acceptance of the problem drinking and permit it to continue. If the family does adapt to the drinking, it will develop a strong commitment to the rituals and routines that support and regulate the drinking as well as a wariness toward change of any kind.

Late Phase: Clarification and Legacy

This stage begins when a family member's alcoholism begins to produce major problems for the individual or the family. For example, the family that altered its vacation plans to accommodate the father's drinking was in the late phase. The questions in this stage are: Will the family remain committed to its identity as a family organized around alcohol? Will it continue to accommodate to the drinking, in spite of serious medical, work, or family problems, or will it become a family committed to recovery from alcoholism? What identity will it pass down to the next generation?

Family processes also play an important role in drug addiction and are similar to those described for alcoholism. Research on drug addiction, however, has tended to stress families in which the substance abuser is the child, rather than the parent, perhaps because severe drug abusers tend to experience major problems earlier in life than alcoholics. While parents of drug abusers are often themselves dependent upon alcohol or drugs and the family processes involved are quite similar whether the substance abuser is dependent on alcohol or drugs, the family in which drugs are a problem more frequently revolves around an adolescent or young adult drug abuser.

STAGES IN FAMILY RECOVERY

Families, as well as individuals, face certain tasks in recovery. Bepko and Krestan (1985) have described stages in family recovery. They observe that, since family systems often evolve in ways that support or "enable" the drinking of alcoholic family members, the first step in recovery for the family involves changing the family system. The recovering family will stop facilitating the drinking of the alcoholic member. This may mean accepting the fact that the alcoholic's drinking is a problem rather than making excuses for her. It may mean confronting the alcoholic, perhaps even arranging for a formal intervention. Members of the family who have been "overfunctioning" may reduce the extent to which they take on the alcoholic's responsibilities, allowing the alcoholic to experience some of the consequences of her behavior. For Bepko and Krestan, the first stage in family recovery involves "*unbalancing the family system.*" This may occur before the alcoholic stops drinking and is often a result of family therapy. Other influences may also produce such changes in the family, however. For example, participation in a 12-Step Program such as Alanon may be a factor in family recovery. Furthermore, this stage of family recovery does not always precede sobriety on the part of the alcoholic. The alcoholic may be the first family member to change. Sometimes families do not recover and continue to function as alcoholic family systems even though the alcoholic is no longer drinking.

Bepko and Krestan call the next stage of recovery *"adjustment to sobriety."* The family must rebalance or restabilize itself around changed roles. The alcoholic may now be participating in the family system in new ways. Other family members may have to give up rights and privileges, as well as responsibilities. Participation in AA and/or Alanon is often incorporated into the family life. Many of the assumptions that characterized the family while the alcoholic was drinking may still be present. The family may still "overfunction" to protect the alcoholic, and family members may be afraid to make too many demands on her. Again, families do not always progress to this stage even if the alcoholic remains abstinent. If the alcoholic returns to drinking, the system may resume its original characteristics.

The final stage of recovery, for Bepko and Krestan, involves rebalancing the system to maintain sobriety. In the previous stage the family maintained, in many respects, its accustomed patterns but without the drinking and the behaviors that directly supported it. In this stage, the family develops more balanced and flexible family roles without the extremes of over- and under-responsibility that characterized family roles in the past. Ideally, the family would also develop less rigid and more empathic interaction patterns that permit it to support individuals in completing their own developmental tasks. This, also, is a stage that not all recovering families attain.

THERAPY WITH A FICTIONAL FAMILY

Bepko and Krestan's model for family treatment is an extremely comprehensive one, and I will illustrate it here using a fictional family that manifests all of the hallmarks of an alcoholic family. The fictional family I will use is the embattled couple, George and Martha, from Edward Albee's play, *Who's Afraid of Virginia Woolf?* While most find this play extremely depressing, I have always believed that it ends on a note of hope and that by the time the curtain falls, George and Martha are ready for change. I have always wished I could be the family therapist who participates in this change, so much so that I have fantasized that I receive a visit from them.

In my scenario, George and Martha arrive in my office for an evening appointment that I have managed to schedule for them in response to a call I received from George early this morning. Having been referred to me by his father-in-law's physician, whom he had apparently called even earlier this morning, George asked to be seen as soon as possible. They enter looking tired and rumpled and sit down together on the couch. Martha is a large, attractive woman in her early 50s who looks somewhat younger. George, who is 46, is thin and graying and looks older, so that the difference in their ages is not apparent. After we introduce ourselves, I ask them what brings them to my office. George assumes the role of family spokesperson and, in listening to him, I am struck by the fact that while his manner is self-assured, and even somewhat arrogant, he keeps glancing at his wife as he talks as if to determine whether or not she agrees with him. Martha, on the other hand, seems depressed and apathetic. She ignores his bids for confirmation and stares silently at her lap.

According to George, he and Martha made the decision to seek marital therapy this morning after a drunken "all nighter" that began with a party at Martha's father's house and culminated, after the couple returned to their house with another couple, in a sexual liaison between Martha and the husband from the other couple, a colleague of George's. Along with the sexual byplay, the verbal hostilities between George and Martha had escalated through the night, exceeding in ferocity most previous experiences of this kind, even though their marriage was characterized by both heavy drinking and heavy fighting. According to George, they were frightened by the viciousness of their fighting but even more frightened by the overwhelming feeling of emptiness and despair that invaded them as morning dawned and the fighting died down. A significant component of the painful bleakness they experienced seemed to be related to a unilateral decision by George to end an unusual shared fantasy that had been central to their marriage for a number of years. This shared fantasy was actually a fantasy child the two had invented.

As we begin discussing the fantasy child, Martha comes to life somewhat and joins the conversation, although she speaks dully and with a noticeable feeling of sadness and loss. She maintains that George killed their son by pretending that he had received a telegram reporting the son's death.*

Martha:	You had no right. You had no right at all . . .
George:	I had the right, Martha. We never spoke of it, that's all. I could kill him any time I wanted to.
Martha:	But why? Why?
George:	You broke our rule, baby. You mentioned him . . . You mentioned him to someone else.
Martha:	(Tearfully) I did *not*. I never did.
George:	Yes, you did.
Martha:	Who? WHO?
George:	To our little guest last night. Honey. Nick's wife.
Martha:	(Crying) I forgot. But you didn't have to push it over the EDGE. You didn't have to . . . kill him.

I ask Martha if she often experiences blackouts such as the one she has just revealed. Both she and George look surprised, but they both acknowledge that she often forgets conversations or parts of an evening. Martha says that she never thought of these lapses as blackouts. I then suggest that George and Martha put aside the issue of the fantasy child for a moment and I begin to ask them some questions about their marriage, about other issues in their marriage, and about their families of origin. I begin by asking George what he sees as the problems in their marriage. George refers to Martha's drinking, mentions a pattern of sexual promiscuity, and calls her

---

*Quotes attributed to George and Martha are often appropriated or adapted from the play itself. That is the case with the following quote. In many cases, however, I have attributed words to them that were not present in the play.

domineering and emasculating. Still thinking about her earlier re-
buke of him for "killing" their son, he says: "*You* can sit there
with the gin running out of your mouth and *you* can humiliate *me*,
you can tear me apart ALL NIGHT, and *that's* perfectly all right!"
Martha, who is now fully involved in the conversation, responds
angrily:

> I've tried with you. I've really tried, but it's no use, you're
> just a hopeless failure. I'm loud and I'm vulgar, and I wear the
> pants in this house because somebody's got to, but I am not a
> monster. I am not.

In questioning Martha, I find that she is the daughter of the president of the college where George teaches. She is her father's only
child and her mother died when she was a young girl. Her father
remarried, but Martha's stepmother died very shortly thereafter,
leaving Martha a substantial inheritance. Martha has never held a
job. She felt very close to her father when she was growing up,
although she did go away to boarding school. About her relationship to him, she says: "Jesus, I admired that guy! I worshipped him
. . . I absolutely worshipped him. I still do." During her sophomore
year of college at a very exclusive women's school, Martha ran off
with a handsome gardener's assistant. Her father had the marriage
annulled and, after completing college, Martha returned to live with
her father. Of this, she says: "I came back here and sort of sat
around for awhile. I was hostess for Daddy and I took care of him
. . . and it was nice. It was very nice." After a number of years of
this, however, Martha decided she would "marry into the college"
to provide her father with a successor. There were not a lot of unmarried faculty members available, but eventually, at the age of 30,
she fell in love with George, a promising young professor in the
History Department. Her father approved of the match and was prepared to "groom" George to run first the History Department and
then the college. George held the position of Department chairman
briefly, but was replaced. Martha's father decided that George
didn't "have the stuff." Martha says: "He didn't have it in him. He
didn't have any personality. Which was disappointing to Daddy, as
you can imagine. So here I am, stuck with this flop."

I learn from George that both of his parents died when he was very young. He is reluctant to talk about this. I ask him a few more questions about what seems to be a family secret and finally Martha intervenes, telling me that George accidentally killed his mother in a shotgun accident when he was about 12 years old. Then, when George was just 16, he was the driver in a single car accident that killed his father, who was in the front seat with him.

I then return to the question of drinking and ask Martha whether she has had anything to drink yet today. George answers for her, saying bitterly, "Are you kidding, she never quit from last night!" Upon further questioning I learn that while both George and Martha agree that Martha's drinking is excessive and destructive, George also is a heavy drinker. His drinking, however, is not defined by either George or Martha as problematic. Instead, both George and Martha identify his "lack of ambition" as a problem for their marriage.

George and Martha's situation illustrates the model of familial alcoholism described by Bepko and Krestan (1985). Bepko and Krestan point out that alcohol can create in the person who ingests it a subjective feeling of warmth, relaxation, spontaneity, and self-confidence. To the extent that the drinker, in a sober state, does not experience these feelings, alcohol can appear to the drinker to have a remedial, or "corrective" effect, changing uncomfortable feelings to comfortable ones. The corrective effects of alcohol can be particularly inviting to an individual who feels, in a sober state, as if he or she is acting in a way that is not consistent with how he or she should feel or act. Alcohol has the ability to restore the individual to a state in which the self is experienced as "correct."

Using Bateson's typologies of complementary and symmetrical relationships (1972), Bepko and Krestan show how, as the alcoholic loses control of the alcohol and his or her life, the negative feedback he or she receives from others increases the need for the "self-corrective" experience that alcohol can provide. The alcoholic's relationship to alcohol begins as a symmetrical one (he or she feels "equal to it") but becomes a complementary one (he or she must correct the experience of being one down in relation to the alcohol by attempting to control it).

Drawing on Berenson's description of "wet" and "dry" states

in alcoholism, the authors point out that because the alcoholic feels and acts one way when drinking and another way when sober, "his experience of self, as well as his behavior acquires an oscillating quality." This oscillating, or self-corrective, dynamic characterizes not just the alcoholic, but also other family members, or "co-alcoholics," because:

> Their self-perceptions become inextricably linked to the actions of the drinker, and their adaptive behaviors represent their own attempt to self correct in the face of the feedback generated by the alcohol-affected person. (p. 41)

Bepko and Krestan stress the importance of understanding the manner and degree to which family members do and do not take appropriate responsibility for themselves, and for tasks related to their family roles. They use the concepts of "over-" and "under-responsibility" to describe family patterns in this area, pointing out that the feelings and behaviors for which an individual feels responsible are regulated by that individual's idealized conception of self, manifested in his or her "pride system." The idealized self, in turn, is shaped by the values of an individual's family and cultural system, particularly cultural values concerning appropriate sex role behavior. The idealized values that an individual has internalized, therefore, have a tremendous influence on the extent to which the individual, in a sober state, has the experience of "correct self" and therefore the extent to which alcohol has the ability to remediate the individual's self-experience.

Traditional sex role expectations include the notion that women will be over-responsible in the task and emotional dimensions related to the maintenance of a home and family (what sociologists have called the expressive function), while men will be over-responsible in the economic sphere (the instrumental function). The rigidity of these idealized conceptions of family role patterns in alcoholic families is accounted for, to a great extent, by the tremendous importance of the "pride systems" of both the alcoholic and the co-alcoholic. Bepko and Krestan derive their notion of pride systems from Karen Horney's (1950) notion of "neurotic pride" (an idealized self-image which an individual develops to feel powerful in the context of deep feelings of anxiety and powerlessness) and from Bateson's (1972) discussion of the role of pride in the alcoholic's complementary struggle with alcohol. Pride systems are especially important in alcoholic families because alcoholic drinking so often results in negative consequences that damage the self-esteem of the alcoholic and of other family members. The greater the gap between the real and the idealized self, the more rigid the pride system becomes and the more drinking is employed to provide the experience of a correct self. Drinking on the part of the alcoholic can correct both the self-experience of the alcoholic and of the co-alcoholic because it adjusts the behavior and the expectations of each. Bepko and Krestan argue that these adjustments may enable family members to repress unacceptable feelings and behaviors or to bypass their pride systems and express feelings and behaviors that are discrepant with their culturally defined sex roles without experiencing the subjective discomfort that would otherwise follow. The following chart, which I have prepared to summarize Bepko and Krestan's discussion of this topic, shows how they see alcoholic drinking as functioning for alcoholics and co-alcoholics of each sex.

Corrective Function of Alcohol for Sex Roles

	Male	*Female*
Alcoholic	Permits emotional dependency while maintaining an illusion of masculinity and control of the relationship	Permits such masculine behaviors as anger, aggressiveness, belligerence, and "independence" within the context of a feminine self-concept. May also aid in suppressing "masculine" feelings
Co-alcoholic	Permits assumption of "female" caretaking role without interfering with masculine self-image	Increases power in the relationship without any affront to feminine self-image

Bepko and Krestan present a list of questions that can be used as a guide to the assessment of alcoholic families. By the end of my

first session with George and Martha, I have gathered enough information to begin to answer these questions:

1. *Where is the alcoholism?* While neither George nor Martha
use the word "alcoholism" in the initial interview, both agree that
Martha has a drinking problem. Martha is a daily drinker, beginning alone at home during the day and continuing through the evening when she is joined by George. For Martha, drinking is associated with marked behavior changes. During the day, her drinking is
associated with apathy and isolation; in the evening, it enables her
to express both her anger and her sexuality freely. George is also an
extremely heavy drinker, although he does not drink in the daytime
and his drinking is not associated with such obviously dysfunctional
behavior.

2. *Who is most affected by the drinking?* Martha's drinking and
George's symmetrical responses to her verbal attacks repeatedly
lead to escalating hostility. Brief periods of remorse and even tenderness often follow "the morning after." In fact, it was a runaway
version of this cycle of drunkenness, hostility, and remorse that
brought them to my office this evening. It is impossible to say
which partner is more affected by this pattern, since it organizes
patterns of intimacy and distance for both of them and allows both
of them to express feelings and behaviors that would otherwise be
unacceptable. It is also equally damaging to both.

3. *Is it really alcoholism?* In spite of the rationalizations that
Martha's "pride system" mobilizes, she is ashamed of her drinking
and experiences a great deal of remorse over her drunken behavior.
She is afraid her behavior will cause George to leave her. At one
point she says: "Some night, some stupid liquor-ridden night . . . I
will go too far . . . and I'll either break the man's back . . . or push
him off for good . . . which is what I deserve." In spite of her fears
about the consequences of her drinking, she continues to drink.
This alone is indicative of alcoholism. In fact, one definition of
alcoholism is that it is "a disease in which the person's use of alcohol continues despite problems it causes in any area of life (Kinney
and Leaton, 1982). Also, Martha experiences blackouts, and drinks

alone and in the morning, all classic signs of alcoholism, George's case is less clear to me. He is a heavy drinker but not clearly alcoholic. I feel that the nature of his drinking will clarify itself as we deal with Martha's drinking.

4. *In what phase is the drinking behavior?* Using Jellinek's (1960) stages, I classify Martha as being in the "crucial" or "transitional" phase of alcoholism. This phase marks the transition from the early stages of alcoholism to the final or "chronic" phase. During this phase a drinker may continue to function with some degree of competence but lives a life that is centered on alcohol and characterized by frequent lack of control over where, when, and how much to drink. Morning drinking, drinking alone, and blackouts are common.[1]

5. *What phase is the family in?* By this, Bepko and Krestan mean, how organized is the family around the behavior of the alcoholic? George's behavior at this time is largely organized around Martha's drinking and its consequences. Their life seems to be dominated by the oscillating pattern that Bepko and Krestan describe. In the "wet" state, both George and Martha are able to express their anger toward one another and to act out gender inappropriate behaviors (sexual promiscuity and neglect of domestic responsibilities in Martha's case and co-alcoholic caretaking and socio-emotional over-responsibility for George). Their "dry" periods, which are becoming less and less common, are periods in which tension builds up, only to be released in an episode of drinking that results in fighting and, in many cases, a reconciliation the morning after. George and Martha are organized around alcohol in the sense that, as Bepko and Krestan put it, "Alcohol use becomes the family's major mechanism for problem solving and 'blunts' the normal developmental progressions of the family and its members" (p. 75).

6. *What phase of the life cycle is the family/drinker in?* George and Martha are at a stage in their family life cycle that Carter and McGoldrick (1980) call "launching children and moving on," although, in George and Martha's case, the child is a fantasy child and the child, who was away at college, dies. In some sense, how-

ever, their creation of a fantasy child is not so different from what can occur in a dysfunctional family with a real child. The fantasy child is a persistent theme in Albee's plays and one might ask whether all children who serve to protect parents from facing their own issues are not fantasy children, at least for their parents. To launch a child, when this is the case, is to experience a kind of death.[2] George and Martha each use the fantasy child to protect their own "pride systems" and to attack the pride system of the other. Since each can only be right if the other is wrong, they must each confirm themselves by refusing to confirm that the other is what the other wants to be. It is this dynamic that produces the symmetrical escalations they experience when they fight. George wants to be confirmed in his manhood and Martha refuses — she is castrating. To confirm George in his manhood would be to admit that her inability to have children is her fault, not his, and she cannot admit that because she needs to protect her image of herself as a good woman. George cannot see her as a good woman because it would threaten his identity as a man. In inventing the fantasy child they have developed a weapon which each uses to bolster his or her own pride system through attacking the other. When they fight about their son, Martha insists that the child is ashamed of his father for being so weak and unmanly. George insists that the child is repulsed by his mother because she is seductive and perverse. If they had had real children, they would no doubt have used a real child as readily as they use their fantasy child. In this case, before they could deal with their own issues, they would have to "kill" the fantasy they had attached to their own child.

George and Martha have also failed to deal with an important task in their marriage. Being unable to have children (a failure George blames on Martha), they must come to terms with their anger and loss, but alcohol (along with the invented child) has prevented them from working through these issues. Instead, their pride systems keep them locked in a battle over whose fault it was and over who would have been a better parent if they had been able to have children.

7. *How does the family "think" about the drinking?* Neither George nor Martha denies that Martha drinks. Martha, however,

attributes her drinking to her unhappiness and her failed ambitions for her husband and their life. And George, also, fails to see Martha's drinking as a primary issue — a behavior that facilitates her expression of other, dysfunctional behaviors.

8. *What solutions have already been attempted by the family?* Neither George nor Martha has ever attended an Alcoholics Anonymous or Alanon meeting, nor has either one been in a therapeutic situation where the therapist identified alcoholism as a primary issue. Their attempts to solve their problems have consisted of "more of the same" (Watzlawick, Weakland, and Fisch, 1974). Mainly, each attempts to build himself or herself up by tearing the other down, using alcohol both to fuel their battles and to numb their pain. They have come to me at this time, however, because they have "hit bottom" as far as their alcoholic system is concerned. They see no hope or options within that system and yet they don't know how to change.

9. *What does the "secrecy map" look like?* Martha's drinking and sexual promiscuity as well as George and Martha's marital problems are an open secret in the small college community where they live. No one would dare confront either George or Martha on these issues, however, because Martha is the daughter of the president of New Carthage College and most residents of New Carthage depend directly or indirectly upon the college for their livelihood. Moreover, heavy drinking is not considered unusual in this community and, as George notes, "Musical beds is the faculty sport around here." As a result, George and Martha's problems are widely noted but never mentioned to them.

10. *What is the family history of alcoholism?* Martha's father can do no wrong in her eyes and she denies that he could possibly have any kind of a problem with alcohol. George is more skeptical, referring to Martha's father's parties as his "Saturday night orgies." Because Martha's mother died when she was very young and because George also lost his parents when he was young, neither can provide any other information about their family alcoholism histories.

11. *What are the patterns of over- and under-responsibility?* Martha is over-responsible emotionally where her father is concerned and also socially, in that she takes a major responsibility for her father's parties and other college social occasions. (George refers to her as her father's "right ball, so to speak.") This over-responsibility where her family of origin is concerned is balanced by a pattern of emotional and functional under-responsibility in her own home. A true co-alcoholic, George is functionally over-responsible with respect to domestic and socio-emotional tasks in the family. Both George and Martha define him as under-responsible with respect to his work because he has not been a "success" in Martha's terms but, in fact, he does function responsibly with respect to his profession insofar as he has a tenured faculty position and meets his academic responsibilities.

12. *What is the perceived power structure in the relationship?* Both George and Martha perceive Martha as being the more powerful of the two. She is economically independent because of her inheritance, she is the daughter of the president of the college where George teaches, she seems to make more of the decisions in the relationship, and she is capricious and domineering in her attitude toward George. She, in turn, is under her father's thumb. In spite of Martha's more powerful position in the marriage, the couple's interactions have a symmetrical rather than a complementary quality. I believe that this is because of the power each wields over the other's "pride system." Also, George and Martha are profoundly dependent on one another and each has a deep fear of abandonment stemming from early parental losses.

Bepko and Krestan's agenda for therapy with alcoholic families is summarized in the following table. Their therapeutic goals and strategies are formulated within a general framework that stresses Bowen theory and works to reduce over-responsibility (overfunctioning), eliminate triangular interactions (interactions in which a third person becomes the focus of tensions between two people), and encourage increased self-responsibility. Within this general framework, they incorporate other strategies at different stages in therapy.

Bepko and Krestan's Strategies

Therapeutic Intervention

Phase	Goal	Strategy Stressed	Specific Goals
Pre-sobriety	Unbalancing the system	Direct coaching and teaching (Bowen), strategic techniques	1. Anticipate and deal with denial 2. Work for abstinence 3. Interrupt patterns of under- and over-responsibility
Adjustment to sobriety	Stabilizing the system	Supportive and structural therapy	1. Keep system calm 2. Address individual issues before family ones 3. Stress self-focus for all family members 4. Anticipate and predict extreme reactions to sobriety 5. Address fear of relapse
Maintaining sobriety	Rebalancing the system	Bowen therapy	1. Shift from "wet vs. dry" dynamic to "correct complementarity" 2. Help couple/family resolve issues of power and control 3. Directly address pride structures to permit new roles without alcohol 4. Help couple to achieve their optimal level of closeness and intimacy

Using Bepko and Krestan's guidelines, I imagine myself having carried out marital therapy with George and Martha.

1. *Pre-sobriety:* My assessment of George and Martha's marital situation convinced me that the issue of alcoholism needed to be addressed first. I decided to approach the issue directly, bearing in mind that, if this approach failed, I could employ one of several strategic techniques. In this case, the direct approach was successful. I told George and Martha that I felt that no progress could be made on the marital issues that they had presented to me unless both partners were willing to abstain from alcohol. Sidestepping for the moment the question of whether or not George was an alcoholic, I stressed the importance of Martha's regular attendance at Alcoholics Anonymous meetings and recommended that George become involved in Alanon. I suggested that if George did find it difficult to abstain from alcohol then he, also, might benefit from attendance at AA meetings. George and Martha expressed a willingness to cooperate on this point. Martha, in fact, seemed relieved. She said that she was aware that her drinking had gotten out of control but had been unable to do anything about it. She was frightened and, in fact, had looked up the telephone number of AA several times in the phone book but had been unable to bring herself to call it.

My second goal, during this early period, was to begin work on the couple's patterns of over- and under-responsibility. I began with some glaring areas of over-responsibility, bearing in mind Bepko and Krestan's caution that it is easier to reduce over-responsibility than it is to counteract under-responsibility, especially in the early stages of sobriety. The first area I addressed involved Martha's over-responsibility with respect to her father, and here I emphasized functional responsibilities (her acting as his "right ball" socially). Where George was concerned, I began with those aspects of his "enabling" behavior that protected Martha from the consequences of her own under-responsible behavior. Much of this behavior had related directly to her drinking (picking up empty bottles and hiding them in the bottom of the trash so that neighbors wouldn't notice them; undressing her and putting her to bed when she passed out, etc.) and was no longer necessary when she became abstinent. George still played the role of emotional caretaker, however, and in spite of his sarcasm, remained anxiously observant of Martha's state of mind and tended to hover over her, particularly in situations where alcohol might be available, as if it were his responsibility to monitor her sobriety.

2. *Adjustment to sobriety:* The relatively small changes in the couple's patterns of over-responsibility that I suggested were very difficult for them to make and resulted in greatly increased anxiety for each of them. In both cases they were able to use their self-help groups (AA for Martha and Alanon for George) to receive support and relieve their anxiety. In a certain sense, the couple changed from being organized around alcohol to being organized around AA and Alanon meetings. This was important because they had left behind two triangular processes in their recovery — one involving alcohol and one involving their fantasy son. AA and Alanon helped to fill the vacuum. My goals for the couple during this period involved continuing to encourage Martha to set limits on her responsibilities toward her father; continuing to help the couple define Martha's sobriety as her own responsibility; and helping both George and Martha to focus on their own needs within the marriage and outside the marriage. While I continued to see the couple occasionally during this period, the treatment plan I arranged stressed group rather than marital therapy for both George and Martha. I placed them in separate groups to facilitate their differentiation from one another, but each was in a group composed of both recovering alcoholics and co-alcoholics, as recommended by Bepko and Krestan, so that they could each be exposed to a range of alcoholic and co-alcoholic interactions and perceptions. Both were in groups that relied heavily on Bowen techniques, however, stressing changes in individuals' family roles rather than changes in interaction processes within the group.

Both George and Martha found themselves at loose ends as they diminished some of their over-responsible behaviors. Martha was so accustomed to defining herself as her father's daughter and helper and George was so accustomed to defining himself as Martha's henpecked husband that neither had any reliable source for enhancing their feelings of worth. Both worked on these issues in their groups and Martha was actually able to discuss with her father her decision to play a far more minor role in assisting him with his social responsibilities, acknowledging that she felt guilty about letting him down and concerned about his disapproval. To her surprise, her father reassured her that his affection for her was not conditional upon her assistance in this area and also told her that he was planning to retire at the end of the school year, in any event. He had put a down payment on a condominium in Florida and would be moving there in the summer. With the support of her group, Martha decided to go back to school and train for a career in real estate. Her outgoing personality, combined with the fact that, because she had lived there all her life, she knew virtually every house and family in New Carthage, were strong assets in this respect. George had more difficulty developing a direction for himself, but with the support of his group, he finally returned to a dream he had discarded long ago, when Martha's father had criticized a novel of his and had forbidden him to publish it. Joining a support group of writers and poets, he began to take up his fiction writing again. His teaching position left him free during the summer and over the long winter break, giving him sufficient time to begin to develop a second career as a writer.

3. *Maintaining sobriety:* About two years after their initial visit to me, George and Martha called for an appointment. It had been about six months since I had last seen them. Martha had recently "graduated" from her group therapy group but remained actively involved in AA. She was program chairman for a Sunday evening meeting near her house and was also active in sponsoring new members. George had just completed the second of his last three sessions with his group. George continued to attend Alanon meetings infrequently — perhaps once a month — and remained active in his writers group. Martha had obtained her real estate license and had joined a local firm, although she hoped eventually to set up her own company. George had recently had a short story accepted for publication by *The New Yorker.* They had asked me to meet with them because, in spite of the considerable gains they had made over the past two years, they were still experiencing stress in their marital relationship. In particular, they had not developed any satisfactory way to regulate their patterns of distance and intimacy without alcohol. In fact, they continued to alternate between "dry" periods of distant politeness and "wet" periods of intense hostility and verbal abuse. These out-of-control fights were often followed, the next

day, by a brief period of tenderness and intimacy during which both partners experienced remorse and vowed to do better. The fights were typically provoked by George's jealousy—he was suspicious of Martha and often accused her of infidelity even though she insisted that she no longer engaged in such behaviors—or by Martha's emotional dependency. Without alcohol, Martha often made emotional and sexual demands on George that he resented. She accused him of hiding away in his study with the typewriter. He accused her of not being able to occupy herself for a minute without him.

My goals for this phase of George and Martha's therapy, during which we met weekly for eight weeks, were the following:

1. To encourage their continued involvement with support systems outside their family.
2. To work intensively on recognizing feelings and developing acceptable ways of expressing anger, encouraging both George and Martha to take responsibility for their own feelings and behavior.
3. To work with both George and Martha to continue developing independence and to admit dependency where indicated without defensiveness.
4. To rebalance the power structure by coaching George to ask Martha to meet his needs.

To achieve these goals I used several techniques recommended by Bepko and Krestan. One technique was particularly helpful in working directly on George's need to always be right. To help George relax his pride system where Martha was concerned, I gave him an assignment in which he was required to make a mistake without explaining to Martha that he was carrying out an assignment. Following my instructions zealously, George spent the next weekend installing a set of bookshelves in their bedroom. Martha had been asking him to put up shelves in the bedroom for months. He purposely installed the bookshelf so that the shelves were too close together to accommodate anything larger than the smallest paperback. Practically none of their books fit into the shelves. George was surprised to discover that, rather than being critical,

Martha was very sympathetic and helped him fix the shelves. Not only that, he found that his sense of self-worth survived the experience of having Martha think he had made a mistake, even though he never told Martha that he had made the mistake on purpose. After that experience, he was often able to follow my suggestion that he occasionally simply agree when Martha criticized him, in order to interrupt the cycle of attack and counterattack. This strategy almost always stopped Martha's criticism and, more often than not, actually elicited her support.

I also worked on George and Martha's inability to express their needs directly by asking each spouse to list the feelings and behaviors that typically took place during their "dry," "wet," and "morning after" phases, whether or not these phases were achieved through the use of alcohol. Their lists were as follows:

MARTHA

"Wet":	I am angry and critical
	I get a chance to flirt with other men
	I don't care what he thinks
"Dry":	He is distant and preoccupied
	He is suspicious and mistrustful
	I feel tense and anxious
	I try to please him
"Morning after":	I can make sexual overtures without being rejected
	He is affectionate and accessible
	We spend time together

GEORGE

"Wet":	I feel justified in demanding to be left alone
	My jealousy is justified
	I feel I have good reason to be angry
"Dry":	She is intrusive and demanding
	I feel guilty for not meeting her demands
	I feel jealous and angry but not entitled to express these feelings

"Morning   She is calm and loving
  after":   I feel sexually attracted to her
               I like to be with her

We spent several sessions on these behaviors, identifying key behaviors that alcohol had permitted George and Martha to engage in without threatening their pride. George's need to justify his behavior stands out, and has already been discussed. For the other behaviors, also, we discussed alternative ways of achieving the goals they were directed toward. The following conversation illustrates this process:

George: For example, last night Martha came into my study three times while I was trying to grade exams. Grades had to be in by noon today and I had a stack of blue books this high (he gestures). The first time she wanted me to look at samples of wallpaper for the guest bathroom. The second time she wanted me to read a letter from her father. And the *third* time she sat in my lap and said she wouldn't leave until I gave her a big kiss.

Martha: (Looking somewhat embarrassed) But you spent all of the night before in your study, too.

Me: So, what did you do, George?

George: Well, by the third time she came in, I said, "Can't you even amuse yourself for a few minutes on your own?"

Me: And what happened?

George: Martha blew up at me. She was holding a bowl of grapes and she dumped the whole bowl over my head. Then she walked out and slammed the door.

Me: So how did you feel then? Did you think to yourself, "No wonder I can't let her into my study—I'd never get any work done?"

Martha: Well, what *do* I have to do to get your attention?

Me: When you go into your study to work, do you ever talk to Martha about it first? For example, could you have told her that the deadline for final grades was today, that you had a lot of exams to grade and that it would probably take you all evening?

George: Well, yes, I suppose I could have done that.

Martha: That's not what he usually does. He usually just goes in there and closes the door and snarls at me if I so much as go in to ask him a question.

Me: What if he did do that? Could you negotiate with him for a time when he could be available to you? For example, if he said he had to spend the evening grading exams, could you tell him that you understood that but that you would like to spend some time with him soon? Could you make a plan, for example, to go out to dinner together the next night?

Martha: Yes, I could do that.

Me: What do you think, George? Would you resent a request like that?

George: No, I don't think so. It would sure make grading exams easier.

Both George and Martha had experienced tremendous early losses. Martha had lost two mothers and George had lost both his mother and his father. George, additionally, had tremendous guilt over his role in his parents' deaths. With the support of their therapy groups, George and Martha had been able to allow themselves to experience the pain of these losses and were often able to see for themselves how these losses had made them particularly vulnerable in intimate relationships. Serving mainly as an educator in this area, I worked on helping each to become more aware of the other's vulnerabilities so that, for example, Martha could see that George's jealousy was not so much a matter of his wanting to control her behavior as it was a matter of his fear that she would leave him. Similarly, Martha's tendency to interrupt George when he was working was primarily a result of her anxiety rather than the expression of specific demands.

I also urged George to establish contact with his younger sister and the aunt and uncle who had adopted her after his father's death.* He had communicated with them only infrequently since that time, feeling that they blamed him for his father's death, and had not seen his sister in almost 20 years. He did write to his aunt and uncle and learned that his uncle had died a few years ago. His sister and aunt, however, were delighted that he wanted to reestablish contact. His sister, her husband, and their two children spent a week with George and Martha over the children's spring vacation. George's sister, who was also a real estate agent, enjoyed spending time with Martha, whom she had never met before. George felt a special bond with his nephews. With a family of his own, George was much more tolerant of Martha's feelings of loyalty toward her father.

It has now been about a year since my last therapy session with George and Martha. I saw Martha recently at a Fourth of July picnic being held by a local business association to raise money for a scholarship fund. Martha took a break from slicing watermelon to introduce me to her nephew (George's sister's oldest son) who was spending the summer with them. Having just completed 11th grade, he was considering applying to New Carthage College and had decided to test the waters by taking a computer course in the summer session. Martha told me that although mild bickering seemed to be a recurrent feature of her relationship with George, their marathon fighting days seemed to be over. She jokingly attributed this to the aging process and a lack of stamina but also mentioned that she had recently celebrated three years of abstinence from alcohol by telling her story at a large AA meeting in a neighboring town. Martha also told me that her father was enjoying his retirement and had been dating an elderly woman who lived in his condominium complex. George, who was away for ten days at a writers' workshop, had been elected chairman of the History Department only a few months after Martha's father retired. His colleagues told him that they

---

*This is the only biographical fact that I invented. The play makes no mention of a younger sister or an aunt or uncle.

would have done it sooner, but they didn't want their department run by the son-in-law of the president of the college.

NOTES

1. E.M. Jellinek was probably the first to conduct scientific research on the development of alcoholism. His studies relied primarily on the self-reports of members of Alcoholics Anonymous and were published in a book entitled *The Disease Concept of Alcoholism* (1960). He described the course of alcoholism from "occasional relief drinking" to increasing tolerance for alcohol, dependence on alcohol, repeated failures to control drinking, and, finally, obsession with drinking, decreased tolerance for alcohol, and complete social and psychological deterioration. Life consequences of increased reliance on alcohol are also described. (Increased dependence, for example, is accompanied by feelings of guilt and memory blackouts, then persistent remorse and failed efforts to control drinking.) While not all alcoholic drinking follows Jellinek's sequence, Jellinek's stages can be helpful in describing the severity of some types of alcoholism.

2. Jay Haley (1980), a family therapist who has studied the process of "leaving home," has observed that when a young person succeeds outside the home it has consequences for the whole family system. The family must reorganize to fill in the gap left by the departing young person. This may be especially stressful if the parents have "triangled" the children into their relationship to avoid dealing with problems or conflicts in the marriage.

REFERENCES

Albee, E. (1963) *Who's Afraid of Virginia Woolf?* NY: Atheneum.

Bateson, G. (1972) *Steps to an Ecology of Mind.* NY: Ballantine Books.

Bateson, G., Jackson, D.D., Haley, J., and Weakland, J. (1956) "Toward a Theory of Schizophrenia," *Behavioral Science, 1,* 251-260.

Bepko, C. and Krestan, J.A. (1985) *The Responsibility Trap.* NY: The Free Press.

Berenson, D. (1976) "Alcohol and the Family System," in *Family Therapy: Theory and Practice,* P. Guerin, ed. NY: Gardner Press.

Bowen, M. (1978) *Family Therapy in Clinical Practice.* NY: Jason Aronson.

Brown, S. (1988) *Treating Adult Children of Alcoholics.* NY: John Wiley & Sons.

Carter, E.A. and McGoldrick, M. (1980) "The Family Life Cycle and Family Therapy, an Overview," in *The Family Life Cycle: A Framework for Family Therapy,* Carter and McGoldrick, eds. NY: Gardner Press.

Haley, J. (1980) *Leaving Home.* NY: McGraw Hill.

Horney, K. (1950) *Neurosis and Human Growth.* NY: W.W. Norton.

Jacob, T. and Seilhamer, R.A. (1987) "Alcoholism and Family Interaction,"

Family Interaction and Psychopathology: Theories, Methods, and Findings, T. Jacob, ed. NY: Plenum.

Jellinek, E.M. (1960) *The Disease Concept of Alcoholism*. Highland Park, NJ: Hillhouse Press.

Kinney, J. and Leaton, G. (1982) *Understanding Alcohol*. NY: C.V. Mosby.

Laing, R.D. (1971) *Self and Others*. Baltimore: Pelican Books.

Laing, R.D. and Esterson, A. (1973) *Sanity, Madness and the Family*. Baltimore: Pelican Books.

Lidz, T., Cornelison, A.R., Fleck, S., and Terry, D. (1957) "The Intrafamilial Environment of Schizophrenic Patients: II Marital Schism and Marital Skew," *American Journal of Psychiatry*, *114* (September), 241-248.

Minuchin, S. (1984) *Family Kaleidoscope*. Cambridge, MA: Harvard University Press.

Steinglass, P., Bennett, L.A., Wolin, S.J., and Reiss, D. (1987) *The Alcoholic Family*. NY: Basic Books.

Wynne, L.C., Ryckoff, I.M., Day, J., and Hirsch, S.I. (1958) "Pseudomutuality in the Family Relations of Schizophrenics," *Psychiatry*, *21* (May), 205-220.

Watzlawick, P., Weakland, J., and Fisch, R. (1974) *Change*. NY: W.W. Norton.

Chapter 5

The Intergenerational Transmission of Addiction and Recovery

Most approaches to addiction treatment take a relatively narrow view of the problem. Treatment is provided to the chemically dependent individual and, at most, to members of the immediate family. In many cases, however, pervasive patterns of substance abuse, chaotic family styles, developmental deficits, and economic disadvantage have been transmitted from parent to child for many generations, sustained by social and economic inequities which appear to be both a cause and a result of these family patterns, and which are an integral part of our social system. Helping professionals working with such families often feel that there are so many problems, each reinforcing the other, that the obstacles to change are overwhelming. At the same time, resources are dauntingly inadequate. Figure 1 presents a genogram that illustrates such a family.

The client in this family was Monica, who entered treatment at 16 for difficulties having to do with a sexual assault that had occurred when she was 11. Monica's mother, Betty, was the first to present herself. Betty sought help because Monica had recently disclosed the sexual assault to her family but refused to discuss it. Betty saw the therapist for two months before Monica agreed to come to a session. Monica has now been in therapy for about seven months, while Betty has an occasional session.

Monica was raped at the age of 11 by a friend of her father's on a court-mandated visit to her father. During this visit her father, her father's friend, and her brother Kevin (then 15) were all drunk. The father's friend told Monica not to tell anyone what had happened and, because she was frightened and thought it had in some way been her fault, Monica had kept silent until the recent disclosure. At the age of 13 or 14, however, she had begun going to wild parties, drinking alcoholically, acting out sexually, and staying out all night. At 16, she

FIGURE 1. Genogram showing multigenerational patterns

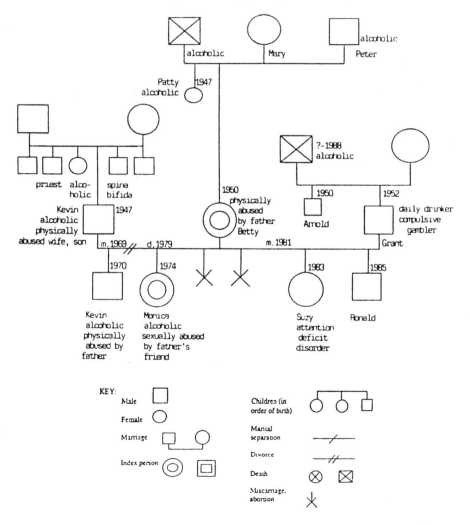

stopped drinking and it was several months later that she disclosed the abuse.

Monica's brother, Kevin, also has an alcohol problem, and smokes marijuana regularly. Monica's mother, Betty, is the daughter of an alcoholic. After Betty's father died, Betty's mother married again, to another alcoholic. Betty's older sister, Patty, is also an alcoholic. Given this background, it is not surprising that Betty's first husband, Monica's father, was an alcoholic. Monica's father, Kevin, was also the child of an alcoholic and has at least one alcoholic sibling. After Monica's mother, Betty, divorced Monica's father, she remarried. Betty's present husband, Grant, is a daily drinker who may or may not be an alcoholic. He is, however, a compulsive gambler.

Betty was physically abused by her husband, Kevin, while they were married. This was not an unfamiliar experience to her because she had been physically abused by her alcoholic father as a child. Kevin also physically abused his son (Monica's brother), Kevin.

Many of these family patterns were reflected in Monica's choices concerning her peer relationships. At 16, Monica had a 25-year old boyfriend, Dick, who was the child of two alcoholic parents and who was jealous, manipulative, and emotionally abusive. Her best friend, Shelley, was also the child of an alcoholic.

This family illustrates many of the multigenerational patterns that can make substance abuse difficult to treat. The genogram presented in Figure 1 also illustrates a tool that can be useful in interrupting some of these intergenerational patterns. Monica helped the therapist construct the genogram and, in doing so, became aware of many of the patterns that had been transmitted from one generation to the next. Viewing family patterns in this light can help a client **recognize his or her** vulnerabilities and can help alleviate some of the self-blame that has detracted from the client's self-esteem.

GENETIC FACTORS

The child of a substance abusing parent is at risk for the genetic transmission of a predisposition to substance abuse dependency. Traits related to such a predisposition, such as hyperactivity or learning disabilities, may also be genetically transmitted. Work on the genetic transmission of alcoholism is still in its early stages, especially the research that is attempting to identify a genetic marker for alcoholism. A genetic marker is a trait that is typically inherited along with the trait being studied (in this case, alcoholism) and that therefore indicates a high risk for alcoholism in the individual with the marker.

Studies of adopted children of alcoholics have been useful in clarifying some genetic issues. Such studies have shown that individuals with an alcoholic biological parent have higher rates of alcoholism than children of non-alcoholics, even when they are adopted by non-alcoholics at an early age. Probably the most well-known work in this area has been done by Robert Cloninger and his colleagues in this country, along with researchers in Sweden, a country that keeps very good records both on alcohol problems and adoption (Cloninger et al., 1988).

The Swedish Adoption Study included 1,775 adoptees, 35 percent of whom had an alcoholic biological parent. The Swedish study has suggested that there may be at least two kinds of genetically influenced alcoholism. The more common, which the researchers called "milieu-limited," or Type I, alcoholism is milder and has a later onset. It occurred in both men and women and, in addition to being less severe, it appeared to be strongly influenced by environmental factors. When children of a biological parent with Type I alcoholism were also reared in a home with an alcoholic adoptive parent, they were twice as likely as children of non-alcoholic parents to have problems with alcohol themselves. If they were reared in non-alcoholic homes, however, their rates of alcoholism were no different from rates in the general population.

Cloninger and his colleagues also identified a second kind of alcoholism, which they called "male-limited," or Type II, alcoholism. Individuals with this type of alcoholism manifested an earlier onset of problem drinking, a history of alcoholism treatment, and a background that included legal misconduct or criminality. Found only in men, and only in a minority (25 percent) of male alcoholics, "male-limited" alcoholism appeared to be relatively unaffected by environmental factors. In families where the fathers suffered from Type II alcoholism, sons were nine times more likely than sons of non-alcoholics to have alcohol problems, regardless of whether or not there was alcoholism in their adoptive home.

While these and other studies have supported the idea that some individuals may have an inherited predisposition to alcoholism, it is still not clear exactly what this disposition consists of or how it is influenced by social and psychological factors, though it does seem probable that there is more than one kind of alcoholism and that environmental influences may have a stronger effect in some cases than others.

Other characteristics transmitted intergenerationally may affect the transmission of alcoholism. Studies jointly supported by the National Institute on Alcohol Abuse and Alcoholism (NIAAA) and the Veterans Administration have shown that alcoholics with a family history of alcoholism differ in a number of important respects from those without such a history. Dr. Elizabeth C. Penick, working with colleagues in the Department of Psychiatry at Kansas University Medical Center and at the Veterans Administration, used structured interviews to investigate the clinical characteristics of 568 male patients admitted to five Veterans Administration alcoholism treatment units during a three-month period (1987). The researchers found that alcoholics with a positive family history of abusive drinking among first degree relatives had an earlier onset of problem drinking and greater severity of their alcohol problem. While this finding seemed to confirm Cloninger's view that familial alcoholism differs from nonfamilial alcoholism, the researchers also found that alcoholics with a family history of alcoholism were more likely than other alcoholics to experience symptoms associated with other psychiatric disorders. Their first degree relatives also were more likely to have psychiatric disorders. This finding raised the possibility that differences between alcoholics with a family history of alcoholism and those without such a history might actually be due to differences in psychiatric status and history. To explore this possibility, Penick and her colleagues studied a subset of 212 men with no individual or familial psychiatric history. The researchers found that, in these men, familial alcoholism history was still related to age of onset of alcoholism, but not to its severity. They concluded that some of the effects normally attributed to a family history of alcoholism may actually reflect the presence of other kinds of psychopathology in alcoholics and their relatives. Their findings suggest that it is important to consider psychiatric diagnoses as well as family history variables in subtyping alcoholics.

As for other traits that seem to be intergenerationally transmitted along with alcoholism, it is not clear whether or not the link between psychiatric disorders and alcoholism reflects primarily genetic or primarily environmental factors, or both. Penick points out that either genetic or environmental influences may be enhanced by the effects of assortive mating. In each generation, individuals with good mental health tend to seek out and marry other individuals with good mental health. Conversely, individuals with poor mental health, either because of mental illness, substance abuse, or both, tend to marry one another, increasing the risk that their children will suffer from genetically transmitted mental health and substance abuse problems. At the same time, individuals with mental health problems may be less effective parents and this, in itself, could contribute to higher rates of mental health problems and substance abuse problems in their offspring. The family presented in Figure 1 is one in which assortive mating has affected several generations.

PRENATAL FACTORS

When such patterns are repeated from one generation to the next, prenatal, as well as genetic, factors may operate. Parental substance abuse can affect prenatal development in a number of ways. First, some drugs can produce chromosomal defects when used during pregnancy. Chromosomes are the part of each cell that carry the genetic blueprint for development, the inherited code that tells the body how to develop. When chromosomes are damaged by alcohol or drugs, they may give the developing embryo, or fetus, the wrong information about how to grow. This can result in birth defects. If the developmental alterations are so severe that the fetus cannot survive, spontaneous abortion, or miscarriage, may occur. Second, both drugs and alcohol can interfere with the development of the fetus. For example, they may prevent oxygen and nutrients from being passed to the developing fetus by the mother through the placenta, thus slowing growth or altering development. Damage to the brain or the central nervous system may result, causing mental retardation or other problems. Third, drugs or alcohol may enter the infant's blood stream through the placenta and affect the fetus directly, acting, for example, as stimulants or depressants. They may have effects on behavior that persist after birth. An infant may be born addicted to a substance used by the mother and show symptoms of withdrawal shortly after birth. Symptoms might include restlessness, irritability, sleeplessness, upset stomach, or even tremors and convulsions.

It is difficult to assess the effects of maternal drug or alcohol use during pregnancy because of the possibility that both a predisposition to alcoholism or drug abuse *and* certain behavioral or central nervous system problems found in children of drug or alcohol abusers may be genetically influenced. In a review of the literature prepared for the National Institute on Drug Abuse, Donald Hutchings has provided an example of this problem (1985). He points out that newborn infants withdrawing from the effects of maternal use of opiates such as heroin or methadone are less alert and attentive than other infants and that, as a result, mother-child interaction may suffer. He observes, however, that it is impossible to determine the extent to which the deficits in cognitive development often observed in these children in later years reflect prenatal damage, early problems in the mother-child relationship, or any one of a number of genetic factors that could produce cognitive dysfunctions, such as minimal brain dysfunction. Such cognitive impairments can be genetically transmitted from mother to child and, if present in the mother, could have contributed to her becoming involved with drugs in the first place.

"Fetal alcohol syndrome" is a name that has been given to one identifiable cluster of birth defects produced by alcohol abuse in pregnant women. Fetal alcohol syndrome includes growth retardation (before and after birth), abnormal facial features, and central nervous system abnormalities such as mental retardation or hyperactivity. Even when fetal alcohol syndrome, in the strictly defined sense, is not present, alcohol misuse during pregnancy has been associated with mental retardation, developmental delays, and various learning and behavior problems in offspring. The effects produced by alcohol are not necessarily different from those produced by other influences capable of damaging the fetus such as other drugs or radiation (Hingson et al., 1982). But because alcohol is the damaging influence that pregnant women most frequently come into contact with, it is a frequent cause of birth defects (Zuckerman, 1985).

THE PARENT-CHILD BOND

Hawkins et al.'s (1986) "social developmental" view stresses the notion of a "social bond." They consider the development of a willingness to abide by the rules or norms of society to reflect a bond on the part of the individual to the social system or the social order. Research on adolescents suggests that individuals who are committed to conventional social groups and organizations also have fairly prosocial values and goals. They tend to have friends who, similarly, evidence a fairly strong "social bond" and they tend to engage in activities that are considered socially acceptable. They believe in the legitimacy of conventional morality.

What are the factors that facilitate or interfere with the development of a bond with society? According to Hawkins et al., it begins with the parent-infant bond. If the early parent-infant bond is satisfactory, and the child receives opportunities and rewards for successful participation in the family, the child will "develop a bond of attachment, commitment, and belief in the family." On the other hand, if a successful parent-infant bond is not established in infancy, or if later parenting is inadequate or abusive, the child may not develop a strong family bond.

A "good enough" parent, in object-relations terms, is one who is aware of the infant's needs and is able to meet them appropriately. "Good enough" parenting begins with the development of a strong parent-infant bond. The bonding or attachment process between mother and infant after birth may be compromised by the mother's use of alcohol or drugs. Maternal behaviors that reflect and reinforce a strong mother-child bond in infancy include such behaviors as: assuming the physical care of the infant, body contact with the infant, staring at the infant, vocal contact with the infant, "mirroring" (empathically imitating the infant's behavior), and comforting the infant. The strength of the bond depends both on the mother's ability to care for the child and on the child's ability to be cared for. A mother who is dependent on alcohol or drugs may be unable to respond appropriately to her infant because of the effects of alcohol or drugs or because she is experiencing withdrawal. If her substance abuse problem is severe and chronic, the mother-child bond may be compromised by potential or actual foster care placement of the child. Upon discharge from the hospital, she may be too preoccupied with her addiction or with her life problems to engage in the behaviors that produce a strong mother-child bond. The presence of any one of these factors may compromise the bonding process.

The infant's behavior also affects the ease with which a strong mother-child bond can be established. The infant of a substance-abusing mother may be born addicted and undergo withdrawal during the post-natal period. She may be irritable, have difficulty sleeping, be difficult to hold and cuddle, and experience problems sucking. Difficult-to-manage infants are less easy to bond with, even for mothers who are not chemically dependent.

Stephanie Brown (1988), in her book on treating children of alcoholics, stresses the impact that parental alcoholism can have on the bonding or attachment process in less dramatically dysfunctional situations. She points out that, to the extent the family system is organized around alcohol, the parent figure or figures will have difficulty focusing on the unique needs of the developing infant or child. The alcoholic parent's attachment to alcohol, or the non-alcoholic's preoccupation with controlling or minimizing the effects of the alcoholic's drinking, may supercede the legitimate demands of the infant or may cause the parent to be so distracted that he or she is unable to sufficiently meet the infant's narcissistic needs for affection, admiration, physical contact, mirroring, or praise. When gratification occurs, it may be unpredictable. A parent who is trustworthy when sober (or when the other parent is not drinking) may be unavailable or frightening when the family moves into a "wet" mode. Some parents express affection only when they have been drinking. Under these circumstances, their affection may be expressed excessively or inappropriately.

To maintain a secure bond with the alcoholic parent, or the non-alcoholic parent in an alcoholic home, the young child may learn to reduce his demands on the parent, or to become overly compliant. His "model" or "scheme" may include the notion that his own needs are best served by being aware of and accommodating to his parent's feelings and needs. Some theorists would argue that, when it develops in early childhood, such an attitude is likely to become a lifelong stance. Crittenden and DiLalla, however, have studied videotapes of interactions between 104 mothers and their young children and have found that although many young children respond to maternal hostility or unresponsiveness with compliant behavior, some of these may develop behavior problems as they become older (1988). Compliance may be an initial reaction to harsh or neglectful parenting but may give way to aggressive or non-compliant behavior as the child grows older. The social-developmental model described earlier would anticipate that the strength of the parental bond may be one factor predicting whether or not an initially compliant infant remains so. Another factor might be the extent to which the child is rewarded for compliant, as opposed to troublesome, behavior.

Because Brown emphasizes the role of denial in the dynamics of the alcoholic family, she stresses the fact that one parental need the child often must accommodate to is the need to defend the idea that alcohol does not account for any of the problems experienced by the family. While Brown's observations are primarily clinical, rather than stemming from controlled research studies, they are quite interesting. She believes that the child in the alcoholic family, because of the influence of family cognitive processes and in order to maintain a secure bond with the parent, may actually experience barriers to normal cognitive development. In those areas of family functioning touched by alcohol, parental defenses may require thinking at a pre-rational, or pre-operational level. To maintain the parent bond, or simply to communicate with the parent, the child may be constrained in his thinking. Brown quotes one of her clients as saying "I either go along with the family's beliefs or I am alone. There is no alcoholism or there is and I am out of the family."

Clinical descriptions of the defensive structures employed by alcoholics or drug abusers emphasize such developmentally primitive defenses as denial, projection, and splitting (Brown, 1985; Bepko and Krestan, 1985). Such defenses rest on fairly undifferentiated cognitive operations which massively constrict incoming information about reality. They also are not the most helpful defenses for dealing with psychological stress in a growth-producing way. If the parents in a family rely on such defenses to cope with the stresses caused by substance abuse, then children in the family have little opportunity to learn more sophisticated styles of coping with reality.

A major contribution of the Adult Children of Alcoholics (ACOA) movement is its insistence that even when children receive seemingly adequate parenting, parental alcoholism can interfere with normal development. This is because the preoccupation of the alcoholic parent with alcohol, and the preoccupation of the other parent with the alcoholic, prevents either parent from fully recognizing the needs and personality of the developing child. Though the majority of children reared in families with an alcoholic member do not experience major psychological impairments, the ACOA perspective points to subclinical deficits that may result from growing up in an alcoholic family.

THE SOCIAL BOND

The development of family bond, along with appropriate limit-setting by the parents, helps children develop the ability to regulate their own behavior and to behave in socially acceptable ways. Such children tend to succeed in school, to be rewarded for their efforts, and to develop bonds of attachment to the school. Bonding to school is enhanced by the existence of a strong parental bond and by the ability to become involved in and skillful at school activities — either academic or social. Children who do not have the opportunity to succeed in school, or who are offered the opportunity but are not able to perform successfully, will have more difficulty forming a bond with the school and with the values it conveys. Learning disabilities and behavior problems may affect the child's ability to perform successfully in school.

The middle years of childhood are particularly important in shaping the individual's ability to function within the boundaries and limits imposed by society and, therefore, to succeed in a school setting. A number of authors have emphasized the importance of game playing in shaping social development during the school years (Mead, 1956; Piaget, 1962). In games, children learn to take the role of the other and to participate in complex systems according to agreed-upon rules. They learn to cooperate and to negotiate over rules in a way that facilitates their functioning in the wider society. Games in particular, and peer relationships in general, promote empathy and altruism.

Janet Lever (1976) has conducted research on sex differences in games that children play and their relationships to one another. She found that boys play differently from girls. They play outdoors more often than girls do, play competitive games more often, and their games last longer than girls' games. This seemed to be partly because boys' games are more challenging and complex (compare baseball to jumprope, for example) and partly because, when girls begin to disagree about how to play the game, they are far more likely than boys to stop playing. Lever, like Piaget, found that boys, throughout childhood, become increasingly absorbed in the rules themselves. They enjoy debating and exploring the rules and trying to arrive at fair solutions to conflicts. The girls, however, as Piaget also observed, tend to be much more concerned with relationships among players and tend not to view the game as worth playing if it is causing too much conflict.

In spite of differences in play, peer relationships and peer activities during the middle childhood years develop empathy and cooperation in both boys and girls and help them develop from what Kohlberg (1968) has called the "pre-conventional" level of moral judgment, in which right and wrong reflect one's own needs and wants, to the "conventional" level, in which social relationships and the welfare of the group become the standard for judging right and wrong.

Some alcohol and drug abusers have not progressed beyond the "pre-conventional" level of moral development. Even as adults, they may continue to view life in terms of pleasure and pain with little sense of social responsibility. Some of these individuals manifested markedly antisocial personality traits even before they began using alcohol or drugs. In other cases, antisocial or delinquent behavior developed subsequent to alcohol or drug abuse. In cases where essentially normal development was arrested by the onset of a drug or alcohol problem, such individuals might benefit from the opportunity to develop prosocial attitudes (Rounsaville et al., 1982). Techniques based on cognitive theories of moral development may be helpful in this regard. (See Appendix C for a discussion of moral development and interventions based on these theories.)

Not all children become integrated into peer group activities in middle childhood. The causes and effects of social isolation in childhood on development have not been well studied. Hawkins and colleagues (1985) have shown that research literature supports the notion that affiliation with a prosocial peer group tends to reflect previous success in social bonding and to result in prosocial behavior. Adolescents with a strong social bond are less likely to be attracted to peers without such a bond. As a result, these adolescents experience more positive peer group influences.

The presence of alcoholism or drug abuse affects the degree to which an individual is influenced by peer relationships and other relationships to internalize the norms of conventional society. Researchers have noticed high rates of learning, impulse control, and behavior problems in children of alcoholics. Also, children of alcoholics may have higher rates of attention deficit hyperactivity disorder, oppositional defiant disorder, conduct disorder, and antisocial personality disorder. Such problems may increase the child's isolation or encourage bonding with delinquent peers. Experts still disagree about the extent to which these differences may be inherited (since alcoholics themselves have high rates of these disorders), reflect prenatal influences, or result from parenting styles of alcoholic parents. Karol Kumpfer and Joseph DeMarsh (1986) compared 60 families with drug-abusing parents to 60 normal families and found that the drug-abusing families were more socially isolated, more chaotic, more disturbed, and characterized by more stress and depression. Kumpfer and DeMarsh also found that children in the drug-abusing families were more disobedient at home and school than the children from normal families, had more academic problems, and had fewer friends.

Zucker and Gomberg (1986) have thoroughly reviewed longitudinal studies of the development of alcoholism and have found the following childhood factors to be associated, each in a number of studies, with later alcoholism:

1. Childhood antisocial behavior.
2. Childhood difficulty in achievement-related activity.
3. Childhood hyperactivity or a higher than normal activity level.
4. Weaker interpersonal ties in childhood (in males).
5. Inadequate parenting or insufficient contact with parents during childhood.
6. Parents who do not present role models of normal behavior (e.g., parents who are themselves alcoholic, antisocial, or sexually deviant).

PEER INFLUENCES

Zucker and Gomberg emphasize that environmental influences may have different effects, depending on the child's personality and the point in the child's development at which they occur. These authors also stress that current peer influences may have a strong effect on an individual's drinking practices regardless of the child's personality or family background.

Peer influences strongly affect both experimentation with drugs and drug abuse. Early initiation into drug use is associated with later drug abuse, but Hawkins et al. (1985) feel that a strong social bond (bond to parents and school) can mitigate peer influences in many cases. First of all, adolescents with a strong bond to parents and the social order will be less likely to be attracted to peers without such a bond (e.g., drug abusers). If they do associate with drug-using peers, they will be less apt to use drugs themselves. If they do use drugs, they will use them less or over a shorter period of time.

Hawkins et al. suggest that adolescent experimentation with drugs may be a form of adolescent risk-taking and identity definition that can occur even in the presence of a strong social bond, especially when drugs are widely accepted and used in the peer culture. Drug abuse or dependence, however, is less likely when a strong social bond is present.

They feel that preventive interventions targeted at preventing drug abuse in children and adolescence should take into account the child's developmental stage. They argue that interventions that seek to increase the likelihood of social bonding to the family through changes in the family system are appropriate from early childhood through early adolescence. Interventions that seek to increase the likelihood of social bonding to school through changes in the school system or interventions that directly affect the development of cognitive and interpersonal skills are appropriate from the point of school entry. Interventions that seek to increase social bonding to prosocial peers by increasing opportunities and rewards for positive peer interaction and helping young people to develop interpersonal skills are appropriate in early and later adolescence.

THE SOCIAL-DEVELOPMENTAL MODEL

The social-developmental model described above is summarized in Figure 2. In this model, infants who have the opportunity to develop a parental bond, who have the ability to do it, and who find the experience rewarding, will develop such a bond. Ability, opportunity, and rewards are seen as factors that facilitate the formation of the bond. Experiencing a successful parent-infant bond increases the probability that a child will have the ability to form a bond with the family system in general and will identify with the family values. The more opportunity that a child has to form such a bond, and the more consistently he or she is rewarded for participating in the family system, the more likely it is that such a bond will occur. Involvement with the family, particularly when the family is characterized by "prosocial" rather than "antisocial" values, promotes involvement in school, although this may be problematic if facilitating factors are not also present (e.g., the child must have the ability and opportunity to succeed in school and must be rewarded for involvement in the school). When both a family bond and a school bond exist, and when family values and behaviors are prosocial, there is a strong probability that the child will be motivated to bond with prosocial rather than antisocial peers, although, again, facili-

FIGURE 2. Social-Developmental Model

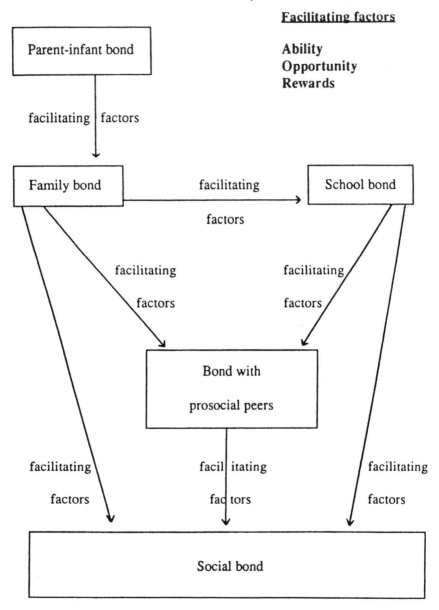

Adapted from Hawkins et al.

tating factors may influence the likelihood that this bond is formed. Positive bonds with family, school, and peers in turn facilitate the development of a positive bond with society in general and the conventional moral order.

Karol Kumpfer, who also sees the development of addictions in social developmental terms, has developed a comprehensive model for intervention with children and their families. Based on research with over 260 families, and an experimental project with parents at a methadone maintenance clinic, Kumpfer has developed the "Strengthening Families Program." This program is a family-based intervention that teaches parenting skills to parents, prosocial skills to children, and gives both the opportunity to practice their skills in a group setting.

Kumpfer's program, and others based on a social-developmental model, stress interventions aimed at increasing children's abilities to succeed within the family and the school and creating opportunities for involvement and success within these systems. For example, they may work to develop:

• Improved parenting ability on the part of parents
• Increased social skills on the part of children
• Perceived rewards for interaction with prosocial children and adults
• Perceived rewards for involvement in legal activities
• Attachment to teachers, parents, and peers
• Commitment to school
• Belief in the moral order

Such intervention programs show considerable promise in interrupting intergenerational patterns of substance abuse.

REFERENCES

Bepko, C. and Krestan, J.A. (1985) *The Responsibility Trap*. NY: The Free Press.
Brown, S. (1988) *Treating Adult Children of Alcoholics*. NY: John Wiley & Sons.
Cloninger, C.R., Reich, T., Sigvardsson, S., von Knorring, A., and Bohman, M. (1988) "Effects of Changes in Alcohol Use Between Generations on Inheri-

tance of Alcohol Abuse," *Alcoholism: Origins and Outcome*, R.M. Rose and J. Barrett, eds. NY: Raven Press.

Crittenden, P.M. and DiLalla, D.L. (1988), "Compulsive Compliance: The Development of an Inhibitory Coping Strategy in Infancy," *Journal of Abnormal Child Psychology, 16*, 4, 585-599.

Hawkins, J.D., Lishner, D.M., Catalano, R.F., and Howard, M.O. (1985) "Childhood Predictors of Adolescent Substance Abuse: Toward an Empirically Grounded Theory," in *Childhood and Chemical Abuse*, S. Griswold-Ezekoye, Karol Kumfer, W. Bukoski, eds. NY: The Haworth Press.

Hingson, R., Albert, J., Day, N., Dooling, E., Kayne, H., Morelock, S., Oppenheimer, E., and Zuckerman, B.S. (1982) Effects of Maternal Drinking and Marijuana Use on Fetal Growth and Development," *Pediatrics, 70*, 539-546.

Hutchings, D.E. (1985) "Prenatal Opoid Exposure and the Problem of Causal Inference," *Current Research on the Consequences of Maternal Drug Abuse*, T.M. Pinkert, ed. Rockville, MD: National Institute on Drug Abuse.

Kumpfer, K.L. and DeMarsh, J.P. (1986) "Children of Drug Abusing Parents: Research Findings and Prevention Strategies." Paper presented at the 34th International Congress on Alcoholism and Drug Dependence, August 6, 1986.

Lever, J. (1976) "Sex Differences in the Games Children Play," *Social Problems, 23*: 478-487.

Penick, E.C., Powell, P.J., Bingham, S.F., Liskow, B.I., Miller, N.S., Read, M.R. (1987) "A Comparative Study of Familial Alcoholism," *Journal of Studies on Alcohol, 48*, 2, 137-147.

Rounsaville, B.J., Weissman, M.M., Wilber, C.H., and Kleber, H.D. (1982) "Pathways to Opiate Addiction: An Evaluation of Differing Antecedents," *British Journal of Psychiatry, 141*, 1982: 437-446.

Zucker, R.A. and Gomberg, E.S.L. (1986) "Etiology of Alcoholism Reconsidered: The Case for a Biopsychological Process," *American Psychologist, 41*: 783-793.

Zuckerman, B. (1985) "Developmental Consequences of Maternal Drug Use During Pregnancy," *Current Research on the Consequences of Maternal Drug Abuse*, T.M. Pinkert, ed. Rockville, MD: National Institute on Drug Abuse.

Chapter 6

Developmental Issues for the Professional

Working with individuals or families who have substance abuse problems can trigger developmental issues in the helping professional. Some years ago I attended a workshop on spiritual issues in healing from childhood incest. The workshop was a part of a conference for mental health professionals who were also concerned with spiritual development. The leader of the workshop was a spiritual director who had herself been a victim of incestuous sexual abuse in childhood. The participants were all therapists. The leader gave a straightforward account of her childhood experience of abuse and followed it with a description of her use of journal writing and prayer to deal with the memories of the abuse, which surfaced only after she got married. The anxiety level in the small, crowded room where the workshop was given was almost palpable as the leader described her childhood experience and her healing journey. Many participants who asked questions after the presentation first shared the fact that they were also victims of childhood sexual abuse. There was an air of urgency about their questions. One question, in particular, was asked repeatedly, in a number of different forms, with the same poignant insistence. Participants wanted to know what to say to a client when the client asked "If there is a God, how could that God have let me be abused as I was?" None of the responses offered by the leader of the workshop seemed to satisfy the need of these participants for an answer to their question. It seemed as if they were asking the question, not so much on behalf of their clients, but rather for themselves. Perhaps they wanted to know why God had let them be abused. Or perhaps they felt they had to answer this question *for* their clients. It was clear they were not comfortable simply pondering this ancient and distressing question together with their abused clients.

"THE WOUNDED HEALER"

Thomas Maeder, in his essay, "The Wounded Healer in the Helping Professions" (1990), describes some of the problems involved when an individual becomes a healer without first attaining self-knowledge. Maeder, who has learned a great deal about mental health professionals through studying their children, describes psychiatrists and other psychotherapists as "wounded healers" to point to the fact that many seem drawn to their work because of their own emotional difficulties or painful family histories. When the therapist has achieved honesty and self-knowledge, these motivating factors need not detract from, and may even enhance, the therapist's effectiveness. When these problems are denied, however, the therapist's own needs displace those of the client and the therapeutic relationship suffers.

Maeder draws on the work of Alice Miller, who, in her book, *The Drama of the Gifted Child* (1981), makes a case for the idea that mental health professionals (she discusses psychoanalysts in particular) are highly likely to be individuals who suffer from a narcissistic disturbance, meaning that they lack a healthy sense of self-love and, instead, feel lovable and worthwhile only to the extent that they are admired and affirmed by others. Such individuals feel they must cut off or deny those aspects of themselves that would cause others to think less of them and, because of this inability to be truly themselves, are vulnerable to a sense of emptiness and feelings of depression and worthlessness which they can escape only by securing the approval and respect of others. Work in the mental health profession may meet many of the needs of the narcissistic individual, since therapists are often idealized by their clients. Also, since narcissistic disturbances seem to originate in the childhood experience of being required to meet the emotional needs of parents who themselves were narcissistically disturbed, such an individual may have a special talent for understanding the feelings and needs of others. Their special sensitivity, empathy, and compassion (the "gifted child") may be what predisposed them to being so responsive to their parents' needs in the first place. Through playing the role of what Maeder calls the "family supporter," they have sharpened these skills still further, becoming ideally suited to the role of professional helper. Miller argues, however, that mental health professionals who have not come to terms with the emotional wounds caused by their parents' failure to meet their early narcissistic needs will use their clients to meet these needs, just as their parents used them.

This description of the wounded healer is very similar to the image of the "adult child of the alcoholic" presented in writings on that topic. As Brown (1988) points out, substance-abusing families, because of parental preoccupation with the substance abuse or the substance abuser, are breeding grounds for the type of narcissistic damage described above. The term "codependence" is frequently used in substance abuse treatment settings to refer to the "overfunctioning" behavior that often characterizes members of the substance abuser's family. "Codependence" includes an overwhelming sense of responsibility for the well-being of another, accompanied by a deep sense of being unworthy or unlovable in one's own right. The codependent individual derives much of his or her sense of importance from helping others and, for this reason, may put others' needs first. Like the narcissistic therapist, the codependent family member has been conditioned to be sensitized to the needs of others, but his or her efforts to help are "ego-centric" (in Brown's terms) or "narcissistic" (in Miller's terms). The other is seen, not as a separate person, but as an object to be used in the individual's "continuous attempts to prove himself worthy" (Johnson, 1987).

Therapists with unresolved narcissistic issues may become pulled into the web of codependence that characterizes the family in which substance abuse is a problem. They may find themselves either unable to challenge and unbalance the system or "burnt out" from too much unappreciated helping. Eric Berne described the codependent mental health professional's role in the alcoholic system long before the concept of codependence had become current, in his classic book, *Games People Play* (1964). In Berne's "life game" of "Alcoholic," this role is termed "Rescuer."[1]

THE WOUNDED CLIENT

Stephen Johnson, a therapist and teacher who has written extensively on the narcissistic issues of both clients and therapists, has expanded on a statement by Edmund White (1983):

> Edmund White has written "a wounded part needs a special welcome back into life." It is our job as therapists to understand our patients well enough to provide that special invitation. The words, the timing, the tone of voice, the facial expression may all need to be "special" in order to move through the labyrinth of defenses to that terrible hurt. Paradoxically, however, we must give up our need for specialness, brilliance, and cleverness to deliver this special message. The message must come out of our seeing the injured child in the defensive adult and speaking to it in such a way that he or she can know that we truly see. Our narcissistic needs to be special in doing this seriously impair our ability to do it. Though all our knowledge will be useful in finding the key, it is often found in that spontaneous moment when our informed humanity gently reaches out to that of another. Whatever techniques are used or eschewed in psychotherapy, these are the moments of deepest healing for our clients and deepest satisfaction for ourselves. (Johnson, 1987)

In recovery from the effects of substance abuse, whether the recovering individual is the substance abuser or a family member of the substance abuser, issues from childhood will often emerge, sometimes in the form of mild to severe delayed stress reactions to early parental abuse. Alice Miller (1981) points out that, under these circumstances, the individual needs an advocate in the therapist, someone who can empathize with and validate the client's childhood losses. When the "wounded healer has not resolved, or cannot control, his own injury" (Maeder, 1990), the ability to be an advocate is compromised. Therapists cannot validate in their clients feelings that they are unable to accept in themselves, nor can they tolerate their patients' uncovering of early abuse if they themselves are defending against feelings associated with early abuse in their own lives. As Miller puts it, therapists can "be more supportive in helping a patient experience his or her childhood traumas if they no longer need to fear the traumas of their own childhood or puberty.''

"THE PATH OF THE HEART"

What this means is that healing, for therapist and client, is something of a shared path. John Welwood has called this the "path of the heart." The path of the heart involves opening the heart and being willing to experience the pain involved in allowing ourselves to touch and be touched by the world and other people even (or especially) when we know we cannot remove their pain (Welwood, 1983). This is a path to a higher dimension of consciousness or self because:

> Letting ourselves be touched in the heart gives rise to expansive feelings of appreciation for others. Here is where heart connects with big mind. For we can only appreciate others if we can first of all see them clearly as they are, in all their humanness, apart from our ideas and preconceptions about them. In seeing and letting ourselves be touched by the humanness in others, we come to realize that we are not so different from them (at heart). This gives rise to real compassion, considered by many Eastern traditions to be the noblest of human feelings. (Welwood, 1983)

Openness and compassion involve a detachment from our own suffering, which is the key to spiritual growth. This growth has been referred to by Marilyn Ferguson as the "transformative journey" (1980). In this journey, by detaching from our suffering, we move to a higher level of consciousness and see our pain in a new context. At this higher level of consciousness, we become aware of the narrowness of our "self" as we experienced it before and instead experience ourselves as a vaster, more inclusive "Self," a point of awareness that encompasses a whole interconnected life process (Small, 1982). That awareness is experienced as liberating, both in the everyday sense that we are able to detach from our immediate pain, and in the spiritual sense that we lose our attachment to our own personal ego and consequently become free of fear and more open to participating in a larger whole. Detaching from suffering is different from avoiding or denying it (which are not growth-producing) because they involve first accepting it.

SPIRITUAL GROWTH

Charles Whitfield, a physician who has specialized in the treatment of alcoholism, sees recovery from alcoholism as a special case of a more general human issue, that of detachment. Drawing on diverse spiritual traditions, Whitfield notes that the concerns of the ego and our attachment to the material world have traditionally been considered the primary obstacles to spiritual growth. Addiction to alcohol or drugs, really, is simply an extremely destructive attachment. Because it brings so much suffering, the alcoholic or addict is sometimes precipitated into surrendering this harmful attachment. As a result, according to Whitfield, addiction can be considered a blessing in disguise, or a curse that is transformed into a gift. Because the recommended treatment, or adjunct to treatment, for alcoholism or drug addiction is participation in Alcoholics Anonymous, recovery from substance abuse problems may bring with it a degree of spiritual growth that most are not called upon to achieve.

The frequent reliance on Alcoholics Anonymous and other 12-step programs make alcoholism and drug addiction unique among psychiatric and medical conditions in that they are the only ones for which the common treatment of choice involves prayer and meditation. Spiritual issues are typically not included in a therapist's training, however, and it is difficult for therapists to grasp the benefits of involvement in a 12-step program if they have not experienced similar benefits through some form of spiritual practice. As David Dan (1990) puts it:

> A legacy of distrust still exists between the recovery movement and the mental health community—much to the disservice of millions of addicts who need access to both. Many therapists remain deeply uncomfortable with the spiritual dimensions of the 12-step programs. The insistence that addicts give themselves up to a "higher power" strikes many as superstitious, and as likely to foster emotional dependency as

drugs or alcohol. On the other hand, people who believe that their lives have been saved by this movement often resent therapists for giving so much attention to seemingly abstract psychodynamic issues and completely missing the point that the addict's present life is out of control. They particularly value the spiritual component of 12-step programs that help them face, often for the first time, the painful question for which their addiction had been a kind of anesthetic: Why am I here? What is the meaning of my life?

Therapists who work with substance abusers, by definition, qualify for Alanon — the program for friends and relatives of alcoholics and drug addicts — and can benefit from the opportunity to recognize and heal their codependence, in their work and in their personal relationships. For those who do not qualify for Alcoholics Anonymous or Narcotics Anonymous, open meetings provide an opportunity to learn how members of these organizations have benefited from the spiritual principles upon which they are based.

NOTE

1. Mental health professionals and substance abuse treatment specialists who work with chemically dependent individuals and their families may profit from participation in a 12-step program that addresses the issue of codependency. This might include Alanon, which is for friends and relatives of alcoholics, CoDa (Codependents Anonymous) for individuals with issues involving codependency but not necessarily alcoholism, and CODAHP (Codependents Anonymous for Helping Professionals). The latter, according to the *Recovery Resource Book* (Yoder, 1990), is an excellent resource for anyone working in the area of addictions. Its purpose is to "discuss codependence as it comes up on the job, with specific emphasis on how to avoid making codependent responses to clients and how to prevent workaholism and burnout" (p. 225). Information on CODAHP meetings or on how to start a CODAHP group can be obtained by writing to: CODAHP, P.O. Box 18191, Mesa, AZ 85212.

REFERENCES

Berne, E. (1964) *Games People Play*. NY: Grove Press.
Brown, S. (1988) *Treating Adult Children of Alcoholics*. NY: John Wiley & Sons.
Dan, D. (1990) "Recovery: A Modern Initiation Rite." *Networker*, *14*, 28.

Ferguson, M. (1980) *The Aquarian Conspiracy*. Los Angeles: J.P. Tarcher.

Johnson, S.M. (1987) *Humanizing the Narcissistic Style*. NY: W.W. Norton.

Mead, G.H. (1956) *The Social Psychology of George Herbert Mead*. Chicago. University of Chicago Press.

Maeder, T. (1990) *Children of Psychiatrists and Other Mental Health Professionals*. NY: Harper & Row.

Miller, A. (1981) *The Drama of the Gifted Child*. NY: Basic Books.

Piaget, J. (1962) *Play, Dreams, and Imitation in Childhood*. NY: W.W. Norton.

Small (1982) *Transformers: The Therapists of the Future*. Austin, TX: Eupsychian Press.

Welwood, J., ed. (1983) *Awakening the Heart*. Boston: New Science Library.

White, E. (1983) *States of Desire*. NY: E.P. Dutton.

Whitfield, C.L. (1985) *Alcoholism and Other Drug Problems, Other Attachments, and Spirituality*. Baltimore, MD: The Resource Group.

Yoder, B. (1990) *The Recovery Resource Book*. NY: Simon and Schuster.

Appendix A

Short Michigan Alcoholism Screening Test

Responses indicative of an alcohol problem are given in parentheses after each question.

1. Do you feel you are a normal drinker? (By normal we mean you drink less than or as much as most other people.) (No)
2. Does your wife, husband, a parent, or other near relative ever worry or complain about your drinking? (Yes)
3. Do you feel guilty about your drinking? (Yes)
4. Do friends or relatives think you are a normal drinker? (No)
5. Are you able to stop drinking when you want to? (No)
6. Have you ever attended a meeting of Alcoholics Anonymous? (Yes)
7. Has drinking ever created problems between you and your wife, husband, a parent, or other near relative? (Yes)
8. Have you ever gotten in trouble at work because of drinking? (Yes)
9. Have you ever neglected your obligations, your family, or your work for two or more days in a row because you were drinking? (Yes)
10. Have you ever gone to anyone for help about your drinking? (Yes)
11. Have you ever been in a hospital because of drinking? (Yes)
12. Have you ever been arrested for driving while intoxicated, or driving under the influence of alcoholic beverages? (Yes)

An individual scoring 2 or more points on this test should be suspected of alcoholism. Positive answers to 6, 10, and 11 are, in themselves, indicative of alcoholism.

REFERENCE

Selzer, M.L., Vinokur, A., et al. (1975) "A Self-Administered Short Version of the Michigan Alcoholism Screening Test (SMAST)." *Journal of Studies on Alcohol* 36: 117-126, 1975.

Appendix B

Piaget's Cognitive-Developmental Stages

THE SENSORY-MOTOR PERIOD

The sensory-motor period lasts from birth until roughly one and a half or two years of age. Cognitive structures, or schemes, during this period manifest themselves almost entirely in physical (sensory-motor) behavior patterns. The infant "thinks" with her body, through action in which she attempts to affect her surroundings. At first, inborn reflexes such as sucking or crying are the only "schemes" the newborn infant has. The infant assimilates the environment to these schemes; for example, sucking anything that comes near her mouth. Gradually, learning, or accommodation, begins to take place. The first evidence of learning is a phenomenon that Piaget has called a "primary circular reaction." In a primary circular reaction, an infant does something interesting by chance and then repeats it in order to re-experience or prolong the interesting experience. For example, the child may accidentally grab her sheet, then, equally unintentionally, let it go. When the infant grabs it again, a primary circular reaction has occurred. The act is no longer just a reflex because it has a slight degree of intentionality to it. The infant purposely repeated an action that it originally performed by chance.

Smiling begins as a primary circular reaction. The child smiles at first by accident then, when the parent responds, the child smiles again in response to the parent. Smiling is one of the child's first imitative acts and is an important social act, facilitating bonding between parent and child. The infant at this stage, however, can only imitate a gesture that repeats one she has just made.

By the second half of the first year, the infant has begun to become interested in more sophisticated and purposive circular reactions, beginning to experiment with various ways of producing a desired result. For example, a child may enjoy kicking her mattress to make her crib mobile shake. She may also enjoy discovering other ways to make the crib mobile move and may smile when she is successful. By now the infant can imitate any gesture made by an adult, providing it is one she has already spontaneously made at some point herself. Soon infants are able to imitate acts that they have not previously performed. They are not yet capable of deferred imitation, however, meaning that they imitate behaviors only right after they have occurred. They cannot remember the behavior or repeat it on a later occasion at will.

By eight months of age, the infant begins to develop the important concept of object permanence. Earlier, if an object was hidden behind a pillow, even if it was hidden while the infant was watching, the infant would not look for it. When out of sight, the object was automatically "out of mind." Now the infant attempts to find a hidden object, meaning that he has a mental representation of the object — the beginning of thought. This means the child is also becoming aware that his mother, or other primary caretaker, has an existence independent of him and remembers this individual even when the two are separated. "Stranger anxiety" may appear in this period. An infant who up until now has been quite willing to be handed from one person to the next may become frightened and cry when held by someone other than the mother. This is because the child now remembers the mother, even when the mother is not present and is aware that the mother is no longer there. The child's sense of object permanence is not yet strong enough, however, to give the child the conviction that the mother will return.

During the second year of life, the child continues to solidify a sense of object permanence. The game of peekaboo is both exciting and reassuring because things go away and they come back. As the child begins to learn language, deferred imitation becomes possible because the child can now represent objects mentally and therefore is able to imitate behaviors that are not immediately present. By 18 months, the child can engage in quite elaborate forms of deferred imitation, pretending to drink from a cup, pretending to feed a doll, etc.

THE PRE-OPERATIONAL PERIOD

The pre-operational period is a transitional period between sensory motor operations (in which problems are solved physically) and concrete operations (in which problems are solved mentally). It extends from around one and a half or two years of age to somewhere between five and seven years of age. The learning of language means the child is beginning to have the ability to represent objects or actions internally. The child begins to be able to reason things out mentally and can use language to try out possibilities in her head. But the language is quite rudimentary and the child at this age does not apply logic in the adult sense of the word. Instead, problems are solved through a kind of perceptual or behavioral trial-and-error. Thought in this period has certain distinctive features.

First, it is egocentric. The child can only see things from his own point of view and cannot imagine the perspective of another. For example, a child at this stage can describe what is in front of his eyes, but if he is asked to describe the scene in front of him as it would look to an observer on the other side of the room, he is not able to do it. He cannot "take the role of the other."

Second, the child is unable to "de-center." The child will focus on a striking feature of a situation and be unable to take other features into account. For example, if the contents of a tall beaker are poured, before the child's eyes, into a short, wide container, the pre-operational child will say that the shorter, wider container contains less liquid than the original one. Or, if a fat sausage of clay is pulled out into a longer, thinner shape, the child will say that the thinner shape has less clay in it. What is missing is the ability to take into account both height and width or both length and thickness.

Third, the child's thinking lacks reversibility. He cannot run a series of changes backwards in his mind to solve a problem. For example, in the beaker experiment, the child cannot imagine what would happen if the fluid were poured back into the original beakers. Being able to reverse this process mentally would aid the child in coming to the correct conclusion about the amount of liquid in each of the beakers in the second set.

One of the exercises Piaget used to study children's thinking employed two identically-sized green sheets of felt or paper that represented fields (Stendler, 1964). The investigator places a cow on each of the fields and asks the child if each cow has the same amount of grass to eat. The investigator continues asking this question, first placing a barn on one field, then placing a barn on the other field, then placing more barns on one field, then more on the other. Pre-operational children responding to these questions tend to base their answers entirely on how the two fields look. They are easy to fool. If the barns are pushed close together on one field and the same number of barns are spread far apart on the other field, children in this stage will say that the cow on the field with the closely grouped barns has more to eat, even though they have watched the same number of barns being put on the two fields. Later in the pre-operational stage, children will begin to reason out their answers but still are easily confused by appearances. They may answer the question correctly when there are only a few widely spaced barns on one field compared to a few closely grouped barns on the other, but may start to make mistakes when still more barns are added and the fields start to look more different from one another.

Stephanie Brown (1985) feels that much of the thinking of the alcoholic, particularly where denial is operative, has a premature, pre-operational cast. Logic and reason are abandoned when a line of reasoning threatens to lead to the conclusion that alcohol may be a problem. Instead, the alcoholic thinks ego-centrically, seeing things only from his or her own perspective, and focuses rigidly only on the aspects of a problem that support his or her position.

CONCRETE OPERATIONS

For children in the stage of concrete operations, logic enters into the picture. The answer to the barn problem does not have to be reasoned out anew each time barns are added because every time the same number of barns is added to the two fields the amount of grass will remain the same. The child at this stage can carry out what Piaget calls "cognitive operations." An operation is a "representational act" (e.g., a thought) "that is an integrated part of an organized network of related acts" (Piaget, 1970). Operations at this stage, however, are concrete, meaning that they have their counterpart in concrete, physical reality. Examples of a concrete operation include grouping objects (e.g., by addition or subtraction), classifying objects into logical classes, or arranging objects in a series (e.g., in ascending or descending order by size). Concrete operations refer to tangible entities and procedures. For example, the concept "5 plus 5 equals 10" can be demonstrated with pennies or other physical symbols. In contrast to formal operations, which are very abstract and often do not have concrete referents, concrete operations are practical and can be learned in a "hands on" fashion.

A child who is capable of concrete operations has grasped the concept of reversibility and can use it to solve problems such as the beaker problem. Reversibility is related to the notion of conservation. "Conservation" means that if a change neither adds something nor takes something away from what was originally there, then the amount originally present has not changed, even if other alterations have occurred. A child who is capable of reversing an operation and of de-centering (taking into account more than one aspect of a situation) can arrive at the concept of conservation by realizing that a change in one dimension can be balanced out by a change in another dimension. A change in the height of a beaker, for example, can be compensated for by a change in the width of a beaker, the net result being that two differently shaped beakers can hold the same amount of liquid. In terms of conservation of volume, then, the child reasons that if no liquid is added and no liquid is taken away, then the amount of liquid in the beaker must be the same as it was before, regardless of the size or shape of the beaker.

The child in this stage can make logical groupings of classes and subclasses and can carry out operations with these classes. For example, a child can be aware that he lives in a certain city and that that city is in a certain state. He can answer questions such as: "Does someone who lives in Chicago also live in Illinois?" or "Is it possible to live in New York City and in the United States?"

A child in the period of concrete operations is still limited in the kinds of thinking that he or she can do, however. Concrete operations are concrete. The child at this stage operates on concrete reality, and is not interested in abstracting general principles and testing them in other situations or in elaborating logical possibilities for their own sake. In addition, concrete operations work on a case by case basis, not according to principles. For example, when a clay ball is pulled into a sausage, a child may realize that there is no difference in the amount of clay (conservation of volume) but may not realize that there has been no change in the weight (conservation of weight).

Concrete operations are important in terms of social development because they permit a child to function in larger social systems outside the home and to understand and follow the rules of the wider systems. The child capable of concrete operations can follow a school curriculum and can participate in organized sports and social activities. The child is now capable of empathy, or "taking the role of the other."

FORMAL OPERATIONS

The ability to carry out formal operations usually develops in adolescence, between approximately 12 and 18 years of age. Formal operations are abstract and deal with the logic of the possible or the hypothetical. Science, philosophy, advanced mathematics, logic, and other such intellectual systems represent formal operations at their most abstract and sophisticated. Formal operations are involved in such activities as forming and testing hypotheses, reasoning logically in terms of propositions and proofs, and relating abstract systems to one another to form principles (Flavell, 1963).

Not all adults are capable of formal operations. It has been estimated that only about 30 percent of adults function consistently at the level of formal operations. The majority fluctuate between concrete and formal operations. About 15 percent are incapable of formal operations (Kuhn, et al., 1977). Alcohol and substance abuse may affect an individual's ability to carry out formal operations. Chronic alcohol abuse can result in cognitive impairment that may persist in abstinent alcoholics (NIAAA, 1989). Such individuals may be limited in abstract thinking and the ability to carry out formal operations.

REFERENCES

Brown, S. (1985) *Treating the Alcoholic*. NY: John Wiley & Sons.

Flavell, J.H. (1963) *The Developmental Psychology of Jean Piaget*. Princeton, NJ: D. Van Nostrand.

Kuhn, D., Langer, J., Kohlberg, L., and Hahn, N.S. (1977) "The Development of Formal Operations in Logical and Moral Judgment," *Genetic Psychology Monographs*, *95*, 97-188.

National Institute on Alcohol Abuse and Alcoholism (NIAAA) (1989) "Alcohol and Cognition," *Alcohol Alert*, No. 4, 14.

Piaget, J. (1970) *Genetic Epistemology*. NY: W.W. Norton.

Stendler, C.B. (1964) *Readings in Child Development*. NY: Harcourt Brace.

Appendix C

Moral Development

COGNITIVE PROCESSES IN LEARNING RULES

Piaget was interested in how children's attitudes toward the rules of the games they played underwent a developmental process that paralleled the stages in their cognitive development. To learn more about this, he observed children of different ages playing marbles and questioned them about the rules that governed their game (Piaget, 1965). He asked them what the rules were, how they originated, and whether they could be changed. Children in different stages of cognitive development had quite different attitudes toward rules.

Very young children, in the sensory-motor stage, merely play with the marbles for the fun of manipulating them. They are not aware of rules. By the pre-operational stage, from about two years of age until about six, children begin to watch and imitate specific behaviors of older children who are playing marbles. They follow the rules only so that the other children will allow them to continue to play the game. They are aware there are rules, but they don't really understand them.

Older pre-operational children have more respect for the rules. In fact, they are somewhat in awe of the rules, believing that they were invented by adults and that they are right in some absolute sense. Their primary motive for conforming, however, is still rather instrumental — they know they have to follow the rules to be allowed into the game.

School-aged children, who are capable of concrete operations, begin to appreciate the rules as a system that organizes the game they are playing. They enjoy competing according to the rules. Younger children in this stage still believe that the rules derive their authority from adults, but they also recognize that rules make the game possible. Winning doesn't count when the rules haven't been followed. Children watch each other and object strongly if a rule is broken. Older children in this stage begin to recognize the contractual nature of rules. They recognize that the rules derive their authority from mutual agreement and can be changed by the participants if all agree.

In the stage of formal operations, which begins at around 11 or 12 years of age, children develop the capacity for abstract reasoning. Formal elaboration and codification of rules becomes important and children become interested in rules for their own sake, often, according to Piaget, spending more time debating the rules than they do playing marbles.

BECOMING A MEMBER OF SOCIETY — MEAD AND PIAGET

George Herbert Mead was a social psychologist who studied the self. A contemporary of Piaget's, Mead, like Piaget, was influenced by Baldwin and other "symbolic interactionists" who emphasized the role of language and imitation in social development. Mead described three stages in the development of the child's view of society. He did not actually study games in the detailed way Piaget did, but he used games as a metaphor in describing this development. The stages he described are: play (which he called "playing at roles"), playing roles, and games.

Play

In the earliest stage of social development, according to Mead, the child simply plays at roles or parts of roles. In particular, the child imitates the behavior of the "significant others" in her environment. Parents and other caretakers are extremely important models for behavior at this point. The child imitates not only the behaviors of others, but also the attitudes and behaviors of others toward her. In other words, a child learns to conceive of herself as others conceive of her. So much so, in fact, that Cooley (1902), one of the original "symbolic interactionists," used the term "looking-glass self." Cooley argued that others' perceptions of us are what shapes our self-concept. We learn to see ourselves, as it were, in the looking glass of others' attitudes and behaviors toward us. In the stage of development characterized by play, the child begins to imitate the behaviors of significant others. Language begins with this kind of imitation. A child may imitate particular words, for example, such as "no," and may apply them to himself, telling himself "no" as a parent would, when engaging in a forbidden behavior. Children learn social rules as they learn natural laws, through interacting with their environment and attempting to produce certain effects. Where social rules are concerned, the effects that children produce and observe involve the responses of "significant others" rather than of natural objects.

Playing Roles

When a child begins playing roles, he or she actually imitates particular roles, or constellations of behavior, rather than simply particular gestures. For example, a child playing at being Mommy will engage in a number of behaviors that characterize the role of "Mommy": bathing and dressing the baby doll, setting out a pretend meal, sweeping the floor, etc. A child will play house, play school, play letter carrier, doctor, etc., imitating the behavior of those in his or her social world. From a cognitive point of view, "playing roles" is more sophisticated than simply "playing" because the child is thinking symbolically and has mentally abstracted certain key characteristics of the roles he or she has chosen to imitate. The thinking is still fairly concrete, however. The child imitates only those behaviors he or she has observed and has no real idea of how the roles fit together in a wider system. For example, she may imitate the letter carrier dropping a letter in the mail slot but has no understanding of how the mail is sorted or transported from one location to another.

Young children in this stage may empathize with the feelings of others, just as they imitate others' behavior, but they empathize accurately only when the other is experiencing an emotion they themselves have felt under similar circumstances. The ability to truly take the role of the other does not develop until middle child-hood (Shantz, 1975).

Games

For Mead, the game represents a metaphor for becoming a member of society in the full sense. He contrasts games to play, such as playing house, in which a child imitates, egocentrically, those aspects of his parents' behavior that he has observed and that he chooses to enact. In a game, such as baseball, a child must play a defined role in a larger system of roles. The fundamental difference between play and a game is that the individual playing a game must know everyone's roles and must be able to understand and assume the attitudes of all the others involved in the game, as well as the overall rules and goals of the game. In play, the child must only imitate a single role. As Mead describes it, the child playing a game must:

> Know what everyone else is going to do in order to carry out his own play. He has to take all of these roles. They do not all have to be present in consciousness at the same time, but at some moments he has to have three or four individuals present in his own attitude, such as the one who is going to throw the ball, the one who is going to catch it, and so on. This organization is put in the form of the rules of the game. (Mead, 1956)

From a cognitive point of view, this involves "de-centering," or being capable of seeing things from multiple perspectives; imagining how others might see and respond to a situation (Piaget, 1962). The game involves the beginnings of formal operations and the transition between orienting one's behavior toward significant others and developing an abstract concept that Mead calls the "generalized other" to which one refers for guidelines concerning behavior. Significant others are individuals of importance in a person's environment. These are people whose opinions are important to us and **help shape** our "looking-glass self." As we become older and capable of abstract thought, we synthesize and abstract from the attitudes of those who have been important to us to form a general concept of what is expected of us socially. This, Mead calls the generalized other.

Mead's distinction corresponds to the two basic stages in children's conception of rules identified by Piaget. Piaget called these stages "heteronomy" and "autonomy." For younger children, rules are heteronomous, or seen as coming from others, particularly adults. They are to be obeyed because important adult figures have said that they are right. For older children, rules exist because they are mutually agreed on by participants in an activity. They exist, by the consent of the participants, to regulate an activity. They can be questioned, debated and, if the participants agree, changed, as in a game. Children in this stage have internalized a conception of how the game ought to be played.

THE CHILD'S NOTION OF RIGHT AND WRONG

Piaget's work on rules in children's games led him to be interested in the general idea of how children formulate their ideas of right and wrong. To study this, he developed a technique that involved presenting children with a story about something a child had done and then asking them whether what the child had done was right or wrong. He focused on areas that he expected would be important to children: clumsiness, stealing, and lying. His interest was not in how children actually behaved, but in what decision rules they used to come up with their answers concerning whether an action was right or wrong, because this was an indicator of their level of cognitive development.

To study clumsiness, for example, he would give the children a story about a child who had broken 15 cups by accident when opening a door and another story about a child who broke one cup while trying to steal jam. Then he would ask them which child had been naughtier. The younger children would typically state that the child who had caused more damage was naughtier, regardless of whether the child had intended to do wrong or not. After around the age of eight, however, when capable of concrete operations and "taking the role of the other," children began taking into account the intentions of the child in the story in judging their guilt or innocence.

They would say that the child who broke a cup stealing jam was naughtier than a child who broke them by opening the door.

This same process operated when he gave them stories about lying or stealing. For example, one of Piaget's stories compared a child who gave a man incorrect directions by accident to a child who gave a man incorrect directions to trick him. In the first case, the man got badly lost while, in the second, the man found the correct address anyway. Young children (under seven or eight), thought only of whether the man got lost and said the boy who made the mistake was guiltier than the boy who tricked the man because, in this case, the objective consequences were worse.

Piaget used the term "moral realism" to characterize the moral judgment of young children whose conception of right and wrong was still "heteronomous." Moral realism means that any act that conforms to the law is good. Any act that deviates is wrong. The degree of wrong has to do with how much the act deviates from the law, not with how evil the intent was. For example, a lie is worse when it is farther from the truth. A child at this age might say that telling your parents you got an A when you didn't is less of a lie than telling your parents you were frightened by a dog that was as big as a horse, because "sometimes children do get A's" while "dogs are never as big as horses." Moral realism also involves the conviction that it is the letter, not the spirit, of the law that must be obeyed.

Piaget found that when he asked very young children (up to age six) why it is wrong to tell lies, they said that it was wrong because it was punished. If he told them a story in which a character told a lie but was not punished, then they did not feel it had been wrong to tell the lie. Older children believed that a lie was wrong, whether or not it was punished.

Older children, who have the capacity to "de-center" and take the role of the other, understand the concepts of reciprocity and cooperation, having learned them through cooperative interaction with their peers. These children can understand that there can be multiple perspectives on any situation and are more apt to see rules as reflecting mutual agreement and good behavior as cooperative or socially responsible behavior.

KOHLBERG'S WORK ON MORAL DEVELOPMENT

Lawrence Kohlberg, a psychologist at Harvard, has expanded Piaget's work on moral development, studying adults as well as children. He began his work with a group of 50 males whom he followed over 18 years. Using stories like those developed by Piaget he studied the development of moral judgment in individuals over time and identified substages within Piaget's general periods of "heteronomy" and "autonomy" (1968).

Kohlberg's technique, like Piaget's, involves presenting stories depicting a moral dilemma and then questioning subjects to determine what they think should have been done and why they think it. Like Piaget, Kohlberg did not study moral behavior, nor was he that interested in the judgments people came up with. He wanted to know why they made the judgments they did. One story Kohlberg used was the story of Heinz, the husband of a woman who was near death from a special kind of cancer. A local druggist had discovered a drug that might cure the cancer, but he was charging an outrageous price for it. Heinz did everything he could to raise money but could only obtain half as much money as it cost to purchase the drug. He asked the druggist to let him buy it for less money or to pay later, but the druggist said, "No, I discovered it and I'm going to make money from it." Heinz finally broke into the store in desperation and stole the drug.

Kohlberg would ask questions like: "Should Heinz steal the drug? Why? Which is worse, letting someone die or stealing? Why?" He felt that an individual's stage of development was reflected in the kinds of responses he most frequently gave. Kohlberg distinguished three major periods in development: the pre-conventional phase, the conventional phase, and the post-conventional phase. Each phase was subdivided into two stages.

Kohlberg's Moral Development Stages

A. Pre-conventional Period
   1. Punishment and Obedience Orientation
   2. Instrumental-Relativist Orientation
B. Conventional Period
   3. Good Boy-Nice Girl Orientation
   4. Law and Order Orientation

C. Post-conventional Period
5. Social Contract/Legalistic Orientation
6. Universal Ethical Principle Orientation

In the pre-conventional period, the child is aware that rules govern behavior, but the motivation for following these rules is essentially egocentric and hedonistic. The child's concern is not with whether he is doing the right thing but with what will happen to him if he follows or does not follow the rules. In Stage 1, which Kohlberg calls "Punishment and Obedience Orientation," the child believes the rules should be followed because, otherwise, one will be punished. Along the same lines, if something is punished, it is wrong. In the case of Heinz, an answer in this stage might focus on what the punishment for stealing is: for example, stealing is wrong because, if you get caught, you go to jail.

In Stage 2, "Instrumental-Relativist Orientation," the child is still oriented to his own pleasure or pain, but the emphasis is on whether a behavior meets his needs or not. In this stage a person looks at whether the rewards of the bad behavior outweigh the punishment. For example, someone in this stage might say that Heinz should steal the drug because he loved and needed his wife and without it, she will die. Or he might say that he should not steal the drug because, even if he saved her life, he would not be able to be with her because he would be in jail.

The next period Kohlberg calls the "conventional" period. In this period, conforming to the family's, the group's, or society's rules is seen as good in its own right. While the pre-conventional period is dominated by consideration of whether an action will bring the individual pain or pleasure, this period has more of an altruistic orientation. The right action is the one that conforms to the existing system of rules and laws, even if it is painful or unrewarded in the short-term.

In Stage 3, the first stage of this period, good behavior is conformity to stereotypical images and approved behavior. It is important to be good and nice, to be helpful and to please others. Intentions begin to matter, however, because the child can now see things from the point of view of another. The child might say Heinz should not have stolen the drug because it's wrong to steal, but he did it to save his wife, so it wasn't as bad as if he had done it for another reason. Kohlberg called this period "Good Boy-Nice Girl Orientation." In order for a child to advance to this period, he must be attached to certain people and desire their approval.

Kohlberg calls Stage 4 "Law and Order Orientation." In this stage, good behavior is respecting authority and following the rules. Following the rules is necessary to preserve the social unit for the good of all. In the Heinz story, stealing is wrong because it is against rules established to protect all members of society. For an individual in Stage 4, following the law is more important than loyalty to an individual, and doing one's duty is good in itself be-cause it maintains the social order. Law is based on the common good or the principle of majority rule. This stage marks the beginning of autonomous moral judgment. Kohlberg felt that Stage 4, or perhaps a level intermediate between Stages 4 and 5, was the stage that characterized more adults than any other.

In the post-conventional period of morality, the individual is aware that different societies have different laws, and that right and wrong go beyond the rules of the individual's immediate group or society. Such a moral stance attempts to define principles that have some universal validity beyond the interests of particular groups or individuals. It involves moral judgments that proceed from princi-ples rather than specific rules. There are individuals who do not move on to this period, but for those who make the transition, it tends to occur in late adolescence or early adulthood. It cannot oc-cur sooner because it requires the ability for abstract thought and the ability to carry out formal operations — to reason according to prin-ciples.

The first stage of the post-conventional period is Stage 5, which Kohlberg calls "Social Contract/Legalistic Orientation." Moral be-havior is behavior that respects individual rights. These rights are guaranteed to members of society through a contract among them. This contract can be revised or modified through legal mechanisms and behavior not covered by the contract is up to the individual. An individual has both rights and responsibilities. Examples of this kind of contract are the U.S. Constitution or the Ten Command-ments. In the case of Heinz, though an individual might say there is some justification for stealing in this case, they might also argue that the druggist also has a right to charge what he wants for the drug or that Heinz should not steal because we cannot leave it up to the individual to decide when stealing is okay and when it is not.

Stage 6, the highest stage of moral development in his scheme, Kohlberg calls "Universal Ethical Principle Orientation." In this stage, morally correct behavior is behavior that coincides with one's own ethical principles. These principles are perceived to have some universal validity. They are abstract principles (e.g., the Golden Rule) rather than specific prescriptions or laws. In the story of Heinz, a universal ethical principle might involve the value of a human life, which the individual might hold more important than obedience to human laws. Very few people operate according to universal ethical principles. As individuals whose judgments reflected this stage, Kohlberg gives the examples of such heroes as Gandhi or Martin Luther King, Jr., who felt morally responsible to obey just laws, but not unjust laws.

The universality of Kohlberg's stages has been questioned. Carol Gilligan (1982) has pointed out that Kohlberg's stages in moral development were based on male subjects. She feels that women's moral development is organized less around rules and more around relationships. Others have pointed out that Kohlberg's views on Stage 6 have not been empirically validated and may simply reflect his own beliefs. Studies of the cross-cultural validity of Kohlberg's stages have produced mixed results. Still, Piaget's and Kohlberg's descriptions of the process of moral development can be very useful to the professional who is working in the area of substance abuse. Many individuals with substance abuse problems have missed out on developmental experiences that normally have a positive influence on moral development. It is important to be able to recognize deficits in this area. Kohlberg's stages provide a framework for assessment.

Kohlberg and others have explored how his concepts might be used to teach moral concepts. Duska and Whelan (1975), for example, are two educators with an interest in how moral values can be **taught to children.** They have discussed the implications of Piaget and Kohlberg's theories of moral development for moral education.

The implications for substance abuse treatment are similar and are important for the mental health professional to be aware of.

Duska and Whelan point out that children will be motivated by reasoning which is at their current level of moral development. A very young child, for example, is more likely to follow a rule because of fear of punishment than because she expects some future reward. A somewhat older child might be induced to follow a rule to obtain a future reward but might not be motivated by a desire to please others. A still older child might conform to receive approval but might not be guided by concern for the group as a whole. When attempting to influence a child's behavior, one will be most successful if one gives reasons that are consistent with the child's present level of moral development.

To produce learning or change, however, one must produce conflict. Moral education must take into account the child's current stage of moral development and must seek to create disequilibrium within that stage by posing a problem that the child cannot solve satisfactorily using the strategies characteristic of that stage. This will result in development if it leads the child to ideas one level above his or her current level of development. Attempts to move the child farther will fail, since children can typically understand concepts one stage ahead of their own, but not several stages ahead of their own.

The following table illustrates these ideas. It is based on Kohlberg's stages and Duska and Whelan's suggestions. For each stage it describes the decision rule an individual typically uses in that stage of moral development. This is the reasoning that can be employed to produce conformity to rules in an individual at that level. It also shows the kind of conflict that will lead an individual to the next stage. For example, in Stage 1, an individual is motivated to follow a rule because of fear of the painful consequences of disobedience. To move the individual along to Stage 2 thinking, one might ask the individual to consider a situation in which a certain behavior brings short-term pain but later reward, or in which an immediate reward is followed by later punishment.

Stage	Decision rule	Conflict that leads to the next stage
Pre-conventional		
1. Punishment and Obedience Orientation	Will behavior have painful consequences?	Behavior brings short-term pain but long-term reward or vice versa.
2. Instrumental-Relativist Orientation	Will behavior bring pleasure?	Behavior brings pleasure to one individual but pain to another.
Conventional		
3. Good Boy-Nice Girl Orientation	Will behavior be approved of?	Two socially acceptable options conflict.
4. Law and Order Orientation	Does behavior conform to the law?	Two laws conflict.
Post-conventional		
5. Social Contract or Legalistic Orientation	Does the law serve the common good?	Conformity to the law violates an ethical principle.
6. Universal Ethical Principle Orientation	Is the law just?	

Duska and Whelan also suggest that a key attitude separating lower (heteronomous) levels of moral development from higher (autonomous) levels is empathy. They argue, therefore, that empathy and mutual respect should be stressed in moral education. One technique of developing empathy suggested by Duska and Whelan is role-playing. This can be used with children or adults to help them develop empathy. A moral dilemma can be role-played with participants taking various roles. In the case of Heinz, for example, one participant may be assigned Heinz's role, and another may be assigned the role of the pharmacist. Then they may be asked to change roles. Or participants may be assigned to act out a particular stage of moral reasoning. They also suggest viewing and discussing films that present a moral issue as a way of stimulating moral development. Experiences that require individuals to work cooperatively in groups may also promote moral development by promoting empathy and a sense of social responsibility.

REFERENCES

Cooley, C.H. (1902) *Human Nature and the Social Order*. NY: Charles Scribner's Sons.
Duska, R. and Whelan, M. (1975) *Moral Development*. NY: Paulist Press.
Gilligan, C. (1982) *In a Different Voice*. Cambridge, MA: University Press.
Kohlberg, L. (1968) "Moral Development" *International Encyclopedia of Social Science*. NY: The Free Press.
Mead, G.H. (1956) *The Social Psychology of George Herbert Mead*. Chicago: University of Chicago Press.
Piaget, J. (1962) *Play, Dreams, and Imitation in Childhood*. NY: W.W. Norton.
Piaget, J. (1965) *The Moral Judgment of the Child*. NY: The Free Press.
Shantz, C.U., (1975) "The Development of Social Cognition," in *Review of Child Development Research*, volume 5, E.M. Hetherington, ed. Chicago: University of Chicago Press.

Index